FAREWELL TO TEXAS

A Vanishing Wilderness

Books by William O. Douglas

Of Men and Mountains

Strange Lands and Friendly People

Beyond the High Himalayas

North from Malaya

An Almanac of Liberty

We the Judges

Russian Journey

The Right of the People

Exploring the Himalayas

West of the Indus

America Challenged

Democracy's Manifesto

My Wilderness: The Pacific West

A Living Bill of Rights

My Wilderness: East of Katahdin

The Anatomy of Liberty

Freedom of the Mind

Mr. Lincoln and the Negroes

A Wilderness Bill of Rights

The Bible and the Schools

Farewell to Texas: A Vanishing Wilderness

FAREWELL TO TEXAS
A Vanishing Wilderness
By WILLIAM O. DOUGLAS

McGraw-Hill Book Company

New York / Toronto / London / Sydney

56876

CONTENTS

                                                         v

FOREWORD

The voices of conservationists are more and more being heard in Texas. Committees and clubs are being formed. Under White House influence, conferences on *Beautiful Texas* have sounded clarion calls to action. And the response is resounding. The people of Texas have [indeed] a bright conscience, a love of beauty, and a passion for the land. But there are forces at work that threaten to reduce large portions of that state to the status of Naboth's vineyard. I Kings, Chapter 21, describes the tragedy:

> . . . Naboth the Jezreelite had a vineyard, which was in Jezreel, hard by the palace of Ahab king of Samaria. And Ahab spake unto Naboth, saying, Give me thy vineyard, that I may have it for a garden of herbs, because it is near unto my house: and I will give thee for it a better vineyard than it; or, if it seem good to thee, I will give thee the worth of it in money. And Naboth said to Ahab, The Lord forbid it me, that I should give the inheritance of my fathers unto thee. And Ahab came into his house heavy and displeased because of the word which Naboth the Jezreelite had spoken to him: for he had said, I will not give thee the inheritance of my fathers. And he laid him down upon his bed, and turned away his face, and would eat no bread.
>
> But Jezebel his wife came to him, and said unto him, Why is

thy spirit so sad, that thou eatest no bread? And he said unto
her, Because I spake unto Naboth the Jezreelite, and said unto
him, Give me thy vineyard for money; or else, if it please thee,
I will give thee another vineyard for it: and he answered, I will
not give thee my vineyard. And Jezebel his wife said unto him,
Dost thou now govern the kingdom of Israel? . . .

And it came to pass, when Jezebel heard that Naboth was
stoned, and was dead, that Jezebel said to Ahab, Arise, take
possession of the vineyard of Naboth the Jezreelite, which he
refused to give thee for money: for Naboth is not alive, but
dead. And it came to pass, when Ahab heard that Naboth was
dead, that Ahab rose up to go down to the vineyard of Naboth
the Jezreelite, to take possession of it.

And the word of the Lord came to Elijah the Tishbite, saying, Arise, go down to meet Ahab king of Israel, which is in
Samaria: behold, he is in the vineyard of Naboth, whither he is
gone down to possess it. And thou shalt speak unto him, saying,
Thus saith the Lord, Hast thou killed, and also taken possession?
And thou shalt speak unto him, saying, Thus saith the Lord, In
the place where dogs licked the blood of Naboth shall dogs lick
thy blood, even thine. . . .

No king has despoiled Texas—no, not even the state. The
modern Ahabs take a different form. Some, with notable excep-
tions, are public utilities who have the power of eminent
domain. But where they lay their pipe lines, or construct their
trestles, or stretch their transmission lines rests in their absolute
discretion. No state agency can veto it or control it. An aroused
public is not even entitled to a hearing.

Some of the modern Ahabs are Federal agencies such as the
Corps of Engineers that builds needless dams or locates them
improvidently so as to drown out rich bottom lands and erase
free-flowing rivers rich in archaeology, history, beauty, and
adventure.

Some modern Ahabs are stockmen who have laid waste the
land by overgrazing.

Others are lumber barons who cut even for the purpose of defeating efforts to set aside some sanctuaries in perpetuity for recreation.

Some are vandals who poison historic trees in order to render futile Federal plans to make a park out of a dwindling wilderness.

Some are oil companies who cause salt water to invade fresh-water bayous where wildlife flourishes.

Still others are poachers who shoot the bald eagle, the ivory-billed woodpecker, and the alligators merely for the fun of it.

Others are irate ranchers who wage war on the golden eagle and threaten it, too, with extinction.

Others spray their hardwood forests to kill those species and let the yellow pine grow, even though the spray kills hundreds of migratory birds and poisons the soil and the watercourses.

There are no public lands in Texas; they are all private.

There are nearly 100 state parks in Texas. But the vast per-centage of them are little more than amusement centers, adver-tised not for their nature trails and hiking potential, but for their dancing pavilions. And private ownership in Texas often lacks a conscience. What was once a rich wilderness has been largely despoiled. There are about 12 million acres of forests in Texas. The smaller landowners, thanks to an expanding con-servation education, are more conscious of the value of wise woodland management than the big lumber operators and have a more responsible relation to the earth. Not more than 660,000 acres of forest lands are protected by law against ruthless cut-ting. The latter are mainly in four national forests in East Texas, north of the Big Thicket, where the U. S. Forest Service applies its conservation standards. The large lumber operators in Texas are largely Robber Barons, pillaging the lands.

The people of Texas are aroused against these modern Ahabs; and their voices are beginning to be heard. But heroic action is needed if the shining bits of wilderness that are left in Texas are to be salvaged.

I am indebted to many Texans who helped me find and understand the glories of which I write.

Lyndon B. Johnson, years ago, first introduced me to the wonders of the Hill Country and Judge A. W. Moursund of Johnson City brought these early seminars up to date.

Jim Bowmer and Bob Burleson of Temple guided me through secret canyons of the Rio Grande, led me in ever widening circles to discover wilderness areas from Capote Falls in the west to the Big Thicket in the east, gave me the patience to see the vulnerability of gushing springs we take for granted; and they rendered me countless courtesies.

J. C. Hunter, Jr., of Abilene, Noel Kincaid of Pine Springs, and Paul Webb of Carlsbad taught me the mysteries of the rugged Guadalupes; and Dr. and Mrs. W. E. Vandevere and Mr. and Mrs. James E. White, Jr., showed me the glories of Capote Falls.

Peter Koch of Alpine made me see the Chihuahua Desert in a new dimension, took me to the relic forests high in the Big Bend area, introduced me to the golden eagle and to the music of the canyon wren, showed me the slow magic of sunlight on colored cliffs, and helped me discover the warm hearts of the River People.

Dr. Barton Warnock of Alpine gave me insight into the ecology of West Texas and taught me that the stockmen were often the villains, while the predator they curse was the hero.

Don McIvor of Fort Davis and Gage Holland of Marathon showed me that enlightened stockmen can also be conservationists.

Laurence Walker of Stephen F. Austin State College and Jack McElroy of Lufkin showed me forest management and soil conservation in East Texas at their best; and William H. Spice, Jr., of San Antonio, geologist pre-eminent, taught me much about the Edwards Plateau.

Donovan Correll, noted botanist, spent endless hours explaining the flora of Texas to me and when possible relating it to the plants I know best—those of the Cascades and the Appalachia.

E. Mott Davis and David Dibble of the University of Texas opened their archaeological archives to me and arranged that I should see firsthand some of the ancient sites before the Corps of Engineers arranged for their permanent destruction by the impoundment of waters behind needless dams.

Dempsie Henley and Price Daniel of Liberty and Byron Lockhart of Austin introduced me to the Big Thicket; and Lance Rosier, who walks the woods with the wonder and humility of St. Francis, showed me its mysteries.

William O. Douglas

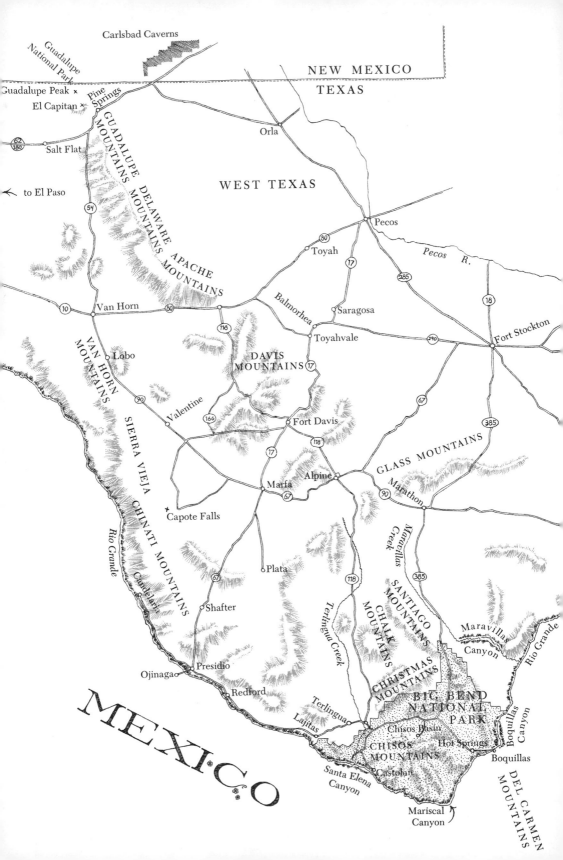

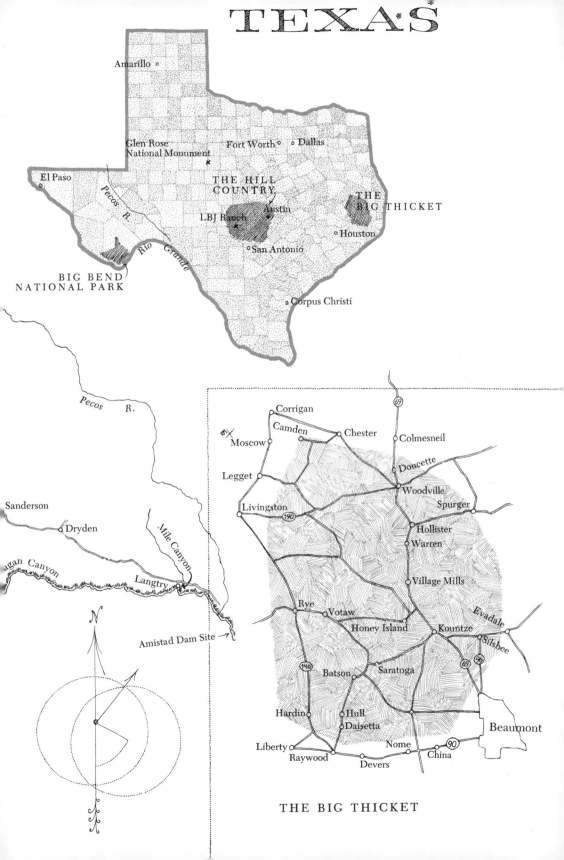

TEXAS

Amarillo

Glen Rose
National Monument

Fort Worth   Dallas

El Paso

THE HILL
COUNTRY

THE
BIG THICKET

LBJ Ranch   Austin

Houston

San Antonio

Pecos R.

Rio Grande

BIG BEND
NATIONAL PARK

Corpus Christi

Pecos R.

Sanderson

Dryden

Mile Canyon

...gan Canyon

Langtry

Amistad Dam Site

N

Corrigan

Camden   Chester

Colmesneil

Moscow

Doucette

Legget

Woodville

Spurger

Livingston   190

Hollister

Warren

Village Mills

Evadale

Rye   Votaw

Honey Island

Kountze

Silsbee

Saratoga

69   96

146   Batson

Hardin   Hull

Daisetta

Beaumont

Liberty

Nome

Raywood   Devers   China   90

THE BIG THICKET

CHAPTER I

THE BIG THICKET

The Big Thicket originally contained more than 3 million acres and was described as the land between the Sabine River on the east and the Brazos River on the west. Today it is reduced to 300,000 acres due to oil drilling, pipe lines, highways, logging, and man's other "development" programs. Trinity River is its present western boundary and it is now confined to Polk, Tyler, Hardin, and Liberty counties in southeast Texas.

This area, not far from Houston, has an elevation between 100 feet above sea level to 400 feet. It is hardwood country streaked with yellow pine—loblolly, longleaf, shortleaf, and slash. The hardwoods include the American beech and the red maple of Appalachia. There are sweet gums, cypress, buckeye, and ash, the latter having eight species, and *Xanthoxylum clava-herculis* or the toothache tree. There are many oaks in the Big Thicket, from the patrician white oak to the scrubby blue jack. On the old Isaiah Fields Farm, cleared in 1835, stands a 500-year-old white oak with a spread that I paced off at 135 feet. The shagbark hickory, familiar in New York and Minnesota, is in the Big Thicket. More unusual is the nutmeg hickory whose leaflets are silvery white underneath. Sycamores brighten many dark bottom lands with their mottled trunks and branches. Magnolia trees

(*Magnolia grandiflora*) are gargantuan. The mammoth gardenia grows 15 feet high with a 22-foot top spread. Persimmon and honey locust are here, the latter having huge thorns on the trunk. Texas has twenty species of hawthorn and many are in the Big Thicket. Indeed, there are at times hundreds of acres where the understory is nearly all hawthorn. Other spots show thousands of acres of the dwarf palmetto, whose stem, when cut open, chopped up and cooked, makes a delicious cabbage-like dish. Different species of holly at times make up the understory. Near Hardin, on the road to Livingston out of Liberty, is a huge holly tree. This is a male tree, tall, symmetrical, broad spreading. How old it is no one knows. But is was there 130 years ago when the land was cleared for farming. Wild plum, wax myrtle, sweetleaf, bay, chinquapin, azaleas, and dogwood often indeed make a thicket. The understory of the hardwood forests is at times so thick that a man on horseback probably could not penetrate it. A man on foot would have difficulty enough. The tight squeeze the traveler experiences in trying to penetrate these dense stands resulted in their being called the "tight eye."

There are bayous in the Big Thicket where the alligator, water moccasin, four kinds of turtles, catfish, and blue heron thrive. It was in the Big Thicket that I first heard of the baygall. I asked Jim Bowmer what it was and he said with a straight face, "I reckon it's a Yiddish doughnut."

A baygall, however, is a Big Thicket name for a small pond where seepage water has collected. It is there that the sweet bay (*Magnolia virginia*), red bay (*Persea borbonia*), and the gall berries (*Ilex coriacea*) are usually found; hence its name.

The bottom lands of the Big Thicket are clay. Larry Walker of Stephen F. Austin State College was with me and he took borings to sample this soil. For a depth of six inches or more the darkish clay was so free of impurities that it was the equivalent of modeling clay. Beneath this upper stratum was red clay which was almost impervious to water. The result is that newly formed pools linger on after heavy rains; the water table is high, nourishing hardwoods. In these bottom lands there are no earthworms, centipedes, and the like that give soil organic as well as mineral content by passing it through their bodies. The result is an almost total absence of topsoil at these lower levels. Leaves fall and are quickly oxidized, the mineral content entering the clay, the rest being washed or blown away. At higher elevations—say 400 feet—there are earthworms, and here the humus slowly accumulates.

The pines *usually* grow on higher ground than do the hardwoods. A few feet may mark the difference; and often the conifers follow that contour line for miles.

I said that the Big Thicket is now reduced to 300,000 acres and is confined to the four counties mentioned. Some disagree with that statement. During my field studies I had several outdoorsmen come to me with a map, showing far-flung pieces of the Big Thicket in other counties. One can, indeed, find scat-

tered spots between the Sabine and the Brazos where the forest conditions typical of the Big Thicket still exist. But they are isolated pockets. The single contiguous area is the one I have described.

The Big Thicket was originally settled in the 1820s and 1830s, mostly by people from Tennessee and Georgia. The land then was Mexico's, which promised 4,000 acres free to anyone with a family who would settle on the land—provided, however, he and his family joined the Catholic Church. Land-hungry people came in numbers, some bringing slaves. Their axes bounced off the hardwoods. Today a power saw fells a 1,000-year-old magnolia in five minutes. The early settlers worked for days to fell one tree and weeks to blow out the stumps and burn the logs. Eventually they had broad fields where they planted cotton. They also grew corn and raised chickens and cattle. Hogs were introduced and they ran loose, feasting on the mast of the hardwood forests. The hogs also loved the taproot of the loblolly pine; then, as now, they dug deep for it until only their twitching tails were visible. The settlers marked the ears of the hogs so that when the roundups were made for butchering in the fall, everyone would get his own animal.

In time sawmills were introduced. They were small operations scattered throughout the Big Thicket and they started the decimation that the large companies continue to this day.

Lumber companies established complete sawmill communities with as many as 5,000 people in places such as Old Fuqua, Votaw, Camden, Greyberg, Village Mills, Pineland—all ghost towns today. The sawmills explain in large part the network of roads in the Big Thicket. Post offices were set up. General stores were built at crossroads.

A Negro once went into one of these general stores looking for a pair of shoes that he could wear when getting married. He had never worn shoes before. The storekeeper had difficulty finding the young man's size. The pair that was closest fitting would not do, because the man's left little toe stuck so far out that the shoe would not go on. They debated what to do and finally reached a decision. The storekeeper took his hatchet and chopped off the man's little toe.

The first oil well was drilled at Saratoga in the 1860s and now the derricks are a common sight in the Big Thicket, as well as wide rights of way that many, many pipe lines have cut across it. The Santa Fe Railroad finally crossed the Big Thicket.

In time the Baptists became the majority and their churches went up everywhere. Near Rye is the Concord Baptist Church, organized in 1845 and attended by Sam Houston. Behind the church and beyond a field where the spiderwort paints the ground blue is Cherry Creek and a baptismal hole.

The Assembly of God is also popular; and there are Presbyterians and Methodists, too. One day Dempsie Henley, when he stopped in the Big Thicket to visit with an old friend, missed the big hound dog that always greeted him.

"I swore I'd never sell him," the friend said. "But a man came by and offered me $100 for the dog."

"Did he pay you?"

"No, he said he'd pay me next week. Said I could trust him because he was a steward in the Methodist Church. What is a steward, Dempsie?"

"A steward in the Methodist Church is like a deacon in the Baptist Church."

The man shot up like a rocket, shouting, "My God, I've lost my hound dog."

The Big Thicket today is a land of God-fearing people who cling tightly to an old order even though schools, power saws, and bulldozers are moving them into oblivion at the rate of 50 acres a day. For decades they rightly assumed that the land was theirs for hunting, whoever might have the title. From the beginning they lived off the land and that tradition continues down to this day. Indeed, not until 1964 were the game laws enforced against them. Now game wardens are on patrol and their job is considered a "dangerous" occupation in the Big Thicket.

Towns such as Saratoga have modern school facilities and teachers as competent as any I know. So in a few decades the level of citizenship will rise and a new generation will realize the awful destruction which the lumber companies, the oil companies, the real estate developers, the road builders, and the poachers have wreaked on one of the loveliest areas with which God has blessed this nation.

The old-timers, however, live pretty much in isolation in spite of radio, television, and newspapers and are sometimes oblivious of the distinction their neighbors have achieved. The Big Thicket has produced five governors of Texas—George T. Wood (1847–1849), Sam Houston (1859–1861), Will P. Hobby (1917–1921), Allan Shivers (1951–1957), and Price Daniel (1957–1963). Price Daniel has a brother, Bill, who was governor of Guam. Both are spiritually very close to the Big Thicket, Price Daniel living at Liberty on its very edge, and Bill at a ranch within the Thicket. When Price was in the United States Senate fixing to run for governor, two Thicketeers were visiting while waiting for their mail.

"I wonder what happened to the Daniels?" one asked.

"I see Bill Daniel once in a while. But no one has heard of Price for years."

I was talking with a ninety-year-old man who evinced no interest in current events, local or national politics, or elections. I asked him if he was a Democrat or Republican. He said he didn't know, as he never had voted.

"Well, what Presidential candidates got your vote?"

He looked at me quizzically before replying. "In all my years no one ever ran for President that I figured was deserving. So I never voted."

The Hightowers and the Lockharts were early settlers, inter-married, and brought distinction to the Big Thicket. Today Cameron Hightower II is in the state legislature from Liberty; Byron Lockhart practices law in Austin.

Ross Hightower is county attorney, Polk County, Thomas J. Hightower is county attorney, Liberty County, and Lewis Buckner Hightower III is a judge in Beaumont.

Samuel Webster Lockhart came to the Big Thicket in 1847 and married Josephine Graham, a schoolteacher, in 1856. Lewis Buckner Hightower came in 1873. He was a Methodist and preached. He was also a judge. He was known as the "Davey Crockett of East Texas" and the "Bear Hunting Judge."

Judge Hightower proclaimed that he was "a bear hunter by profession and a lawyer by avocation." He killed his first bear at the age of thirteen. He would even adjourn court if he heard of a marauding bear. He preferred bear meat over all other meats and prepared a special bear meat sauce which is highly treasured by the family and sometimes known as Hot Catsup:

> 1 gallon tomato juice
> 4 large onions cut up

Let onions and juice boil about 30 minutes.

> 2 tablespoons of dry mustard
> 2 tablespoons of red pepper
> 2 tablespoons of cloves
> 1 tablespoon of mace
> 1 tablespoon of allspice
> 1 tablespoon of cinnamon
> $\frac{1}{2}$ cup sugar
> $\frac{1}{4}$ cup salt

Mix spices, sugar, and salt; pour into one pint of vinegar. Let this mix set for a few minutes, then put the same in with tomato juice and onions and let simmer about five (5) minutes.

"It's best," Mrs. Mary Hightower Davis told me, "if you make your own tomato juice by grinding up fresh tomatoes. Our family usually makes enough of the catsup when the tomatoes are ripe to last all year."

Lewis Buckner Hightower II was also a famous judge of the Big Thicket.

Judge Hightower I had nineteen children by four wives. His fourth wife was Jane Lockhart, by whom he had nine children. Jane's brother, Thomas Jefferson Lockhart, had seven children. Apart from one of them, Lewis Buckner Hightower Lockhart, he named his children in chronological order after the letters of the Greek alphabet—Alpha Omega, Beta Gamma, Delta Epsilon, Theta Iota, Omicron Pi, and Upsilon Phi.

The Lockharts and the Hightowers, having been united, heavily populated the Big Thicket; and while today some have left, these two families are still prominent in Big Thicket affairs.

An unusual criminal case was once presented to Judge Hightower I. A settler, suspecting that a young man, whom he disliked, was visiting his daughter surreptitiously at night, put a bear trap outside her window. Sure enough, the suspect was caught the first night and a prosecution of sorts was instigated. After hearing the prosecutor's evidence, Judge Hightower dismissed the case, saying, "If they're going to use bear traps for this purpose, they might even catch a judge."

Judge Hightower I, who died in 1919, was running for re-election shortly before that time. He was noted for his fondness for alcohol, and an opponent who was "dry" tried to exploit that frailty. Price Daniel's father, also a "dry," came out for Hightower and helped him win, saying that "Hightower drunk" was a better judge than his opponent would be sober.

A Lockhart inadvertently gave rise to a scary rumor that there was a wild man in the Big Thicket. He was visiting a lady friend at night when her husband unexpectedly came home. Lockhart escaped by the window in such a hurry that he left all his clothes behind. He was tall, hairy, and naked as he stalked through the Thicket in the dim light of dawn, scaring the wits out of a few travelers who sounded the alarm that started a futile search.

There are ghost roads in the Big Thicket where at night eerie forms appear and disappear. They take bizarre shapes and sometimes run or dance. Small groups gather at strategic points even to this day to watch them. The phenomena are explained in terms of phosphorescent gases or insects or rabbits who have become impregnated with the gases.

Today no cotton is grown in the Big Thicket, those quotas having been moved west. Some rice has gone in; but mostly the farms are small and diversified, cash income coming largely from jobs in sawmills.

No one has better described the abodes of the Thicketeers than Mary Laswell in *I'll Take Texas:*

> Hound dogs and blowing horns. Blackeyed peas and hog jowl. Sausage, with a flavor unrivaled, red-pepper-hot, solid pork-meat with some substance to it. Grits floating in fresh butter or red-eye gravy. Hot biscuits and mayhaw jelly. Kids selling buckets of haws by the road spell it "may halls". A poky mule turning a syrup mill. The land where *The King and I* means nothing but an old-time gospel hymn. Gray silvered shacks with bitter oranges and chinaberry trees near them . . . the yard a bleached sweep of hard-packed earth, an iron washpot turned over near a round white spot on the ground where the suds from strong yellow lye-soap wash water had been emptied for years. The broomstick used to punch the clothes down, boiled to the color and smoothness of old ivory. Grove's Chill Tonic and Slaughterine for Pains. Crisper's Hot Shot Nerve Sedative.
>
> The country where a midwife is a "granny woe-man"; one a 92-year-old mulatto woman with slender steely fingers who was said to have delivered a live baby from a dead mother. "White doctor say she daid, so I don't say she ain't." Signs saying "Wheels

Spoked." Negro help leaping the fence to "git away fum de
cunjerin' powder on de gate posts," placed there by some
"cunjer" man or woman in the hire of an ill-wisher. East Texas,
where they do things *right*, not cloddish. Negro children shouting "Santy Claw comin'? Santy Claw comin'?" when you want
to take their pictures: "How he gon' know me on paper?" The
stompin' ground of a blind, toothless guitar player: "Play me
some blues." "I don' play no sinful songs, lady." His gigantic wife,
Billie, emerging from out back hollerin' "An' me lookin' like
Who'd-a-Thunk-It!" Razor-back hogs and hickory nuts. Light-
bread and sweet milk. English walnuts and Irish potatoes, and
firecrackers at Christmas. The smell of fresh-made lye hominy,
and the lacquered cypress beams of the smokehouse. A hint of
frost in the air, and the sweet mouth of a coon dog when he
trees.

Supper in the Big Thicket is apt to be sweet milk, hot biscuits,
honey, and butter. The honey is in a deep saucer at everyone's
place. The butter is in a huge common jar and one reaches for
it with his knife. A friend of mine, having such a supper with a
family deep in the Big Thicket, relates how the mother slapped
one of her sons in the face, saying, "How many times have I told
you to lick your knife clean before putting it in the butter?"

Pokeweed (*Phytolacca americana*) has a large poisonous root.
But its young leafy sprouts, many think, are sweeter than aspar-
agus.

"Poke and catfish is about the best dish in the Big Thicket,"
Lance Rosier told me.

Some interesting recipes come out of the Big Thicket. We got
from Mrs. H. L Phillips of Kountze the following one for corncob
jelly:

> 12–15 red dry corncobs
> 3½ cups water
> 4 cups sugar
> 6 oz. commercial pectin (1 bottle Certo
> or 1 box Sure-Jell)

*Cut corncobs in small pieces. Cover with water. Bring to boil,
then simmer for one hour or until liquid has strong flavor. Remove from heat, cover, let stand for ten minutes. Strain through
cloth to make three cups prepared juice. Add pectin, dissolve.
Then add sugar. Boil hard for five minutes. Add coloring to color
bright red. Cool five minutes. Pour in jars.*

"If you want a whitish corncob jelly," Lance volunteered, "use
ordinary white cobs."

A Social Security agent was recently taking a census in the
Big Thicket. He asked one man in his twenties what his occupation was. The word was new to him so he could not answer. The
agent rephrased it several times in terms of work and wages. The
young man finally answered, "Last year I worked in a gravel
pit."

The agent insisted he was interested not in last year but right
now.

"Right now I'm frog gigging."

I mentioned that the youngsters now being educated will turn
out to be a different breed. And so they will. But even today
things common to the city-bred child may be startling or unusual
to them. When my helicopter put down on the lawn of the high
school at Saratoga, all classes broke up and children streamed
out of every door with wonder and curiosity.

Dempsie Henley, mayor of Liberty, has air conditioning in his
car, with the blower on the extreme right of the dashboard. He
picked up a nine- or ten-year-old boy on a hot summer day and
put him in the front seat. The boy was so small that the stream
of cold air hit him right between the eyes. It so bothered and interested the lad that he could not take his eyes off it. When
Dempsie Henley let the lad off at his destination he said, "If I
were you, mister, I'd sure fix that hole in your car before winter.
If you don't, you're going to freeze to death."

There was a hot spell in September when Dempsie Henley had
his air conditioner on in the car. He picked up an old man from

the Big Thicket who, feeling the cold blast, pulled his coat collar tighter and tighter around his neck. After twenty minutes or so he asked to get out and go home. When asked why, he replied, "With this norther coming up it'll be ideal weather for hog killing."

Dempsie Henley, whose great-grandfather, Isaiah Fields, settled near Liberty in 1835, grew up there. "We were so poor," he told me, "that until I got into the army in World War II, I thought everybody else was poor, too."

To eke out a living he collected the Spanish moss (*Tillandsia usneoides*) that hangs from all the hardwoods in the Big Thicket. This moss is grayish in appearance. But that is the exterior. In the center is a small wiry fiber almost as strong as horsehair. That fiber is used as stuffing for pillows and chairs. The Thicketeers collect it. "The stuff is so light that you work hard for a whole week and you won't have even 100 pounds."

Dempsie Henley today is a great civic leader and a conservationist, one of the leading spirits behind the Big Thicket Association, organized in 1964, which is out to save at least islands of the 300,000 acres as parks or sanctuaries. Walter McCreight of Batson has written a stirring song, "Land of the Big Thicket," calling people to action.

Another leading conservationist of the Big Thicket is Lance Rosier, who lives in a small cottage behind the post office at Saratoga. Lance was born in the Big Thicket and has spent all of his sixty-odd years there. He is a slight, gnome-like man who, according to Mary Laswell in *I'll Take Texas*, would weigh 120 pounds "soaking wet." That's about right. He walks the woods quietly and reverently. He is on speaking terms with all that blooms, with all that crawls or swims, with all that flies.

He was considered an "odd ball" by his contemporaries. His classmates taunted him for wanting to search out plants and identify them, rather than shoot birds. The people of Saratoga wanted him to become a "useful" citizen. But the Thoreau that was in him made him turn his back on the town and head for the Big Thicket.

"I sat for hours on a stump until at last I could tell the difference between the song of the white-eyed vireo and the red-eyed one," he told me. He sent away for books on birds and plants and began at high-school age the slow process of classification and identification that has made him Mr. Big Thicket, the outstanding naturalist of the area. I gather that the taunting by his contemporaries and their rejection of him hurt this sensitive man to the quick. His confidence in himself probably dates from his association with H. B. Parks and V. L. Cory, who published in 1938 their *Biological Survey of the East Texas Big Thicket Area.* He was with them in the Big Thicket for weeks on end as they did their field work for this and other books; and from them he received the only technical instruction in botany he ever enjoyed. With their keys at his disposal he went to work in earnest and now knows the common names, and the Latin as well, of the several thousand plants that grow in the Big Thicket.

People are always running to him with a specimen, as I did, and asking, "Lance, what is this?" And he always knows. He not only knows the name but the use, if any, that the Indians and early settlers made of it, and its present commercial value as well. One day a small circus came to Saratoga. Among the animals was a baboon that suddenly died. The circus people dumped the carcass by the roadside as they left town. The next day some local people found it and brought it to Lance, asking, "Lance, what is this?" Lance studied awhile and then solemnly replied, "Judging from the calluses on its rump, the stoop of its back, and the depressed look on its face, I reckon it's a Big Thicket domino player."

Lance told me about the bootlegging in the Big Thicket. It was an ideal place for whiskey making. The principal ingredient was corn, and the product was sold in fruit jars that held a little less than one-half gallon and hence were called a "short half." Steel drums were used, a drum of mash, sealed at the top except for one opening, being fired up. From the opening came a copper tube that ran through a running creek to another steel drum into which the final product dripped. Big Thicket whiskey, they say, tasted not like bourbon but like Drambuie. A prudent drinker, when offered a drink from a jar, closed the lid tightly and vigorously shook it before imbibing in order to distribute the fusel oil uniformly.

Aging was achieved by chopping chips from a red oak and dropping them in the distillate. After two weeks the whiskey was "aged."

In the old days a man by the name of Drew had a general store at Drew's Landing.

"Most honest man I ever knew," Lance told me. "He kept a sign out—Whiskey, $1.00 a gallon; Good Whiskey, $1.50 a gallon."

Even today Texas liquor officials seize more stills in East Texas than anywhere else. And some are still found in the Big Thicket. "Cover is necessary for a still," one official said. "And East Texas woods are hard to beat in that respect."

A few years ago one of the local citizens was brought before the local judge on a charge of making whiskey. This was the fourth offense. The old man's only defense was that he was not a whiskey seller, he only made the stuff for his own use. The judge remonstrated with him.

"George," he said, "the commercial distillers put out a real good product these days, and they sell it at a reasonable price. I know you don't have much money, but it would be far better for you simply to buy a bottle every now and then than to keep on making this stuff and keep on getting caught."

"I dunno, I dunno," said the defendant.

"Of course I'm right," the judge said. "I'll prove it to you. How much do you drink?"

"A half gallon a day for me," said the defendant, "and then there's the family."

The judge thought it over for a minute. "Forget what I just said, George," he said. "Maybe your way is the best way after all."

I traveled the Big Thicket with Lance when the bright leaves of the hardwoods were first showing and the flowering shrubs were at their peak. We stopped at a stand of cypress whose bright green leaves were bursting from the buds.

"Ever see a young mesquite in bloom?" asked Lance. "Doesn't the cypress leaf remind you a bit of it at this stage? Filigree like."

We stopped at a baygall where a huge cypress with many knees grows. While some others in the party undertook to measure it, Lance, with a knowing eye, squinted skyward and said, "One hundred thirty-five feet." And so it was. It was 11 feet in diameter and probably 1,000 years old. It stood in isolated splendor dominating some 20 acres of fairly open woodland. A few water ash, water oak, and elm were on the stand. Pecans and hickories were there, too, but they showed no leaves.

"Dead?" I asked.

"No, no," Lance replied. "They are the last trees to bud. After they bud, there's no more cold weather. You can count on that."

A blue mint was thick and Lance picked a sample to show me how mint always has a square stem. Wisteria, which is native in the Big Thicket, was in bloom, reaching for treetops to put its flowers on full display. Buttercups sent streaks of yellow through the grass. Clumps of vetch were flourishing and wild roses were in their heyday. We sat on a log, drinking in the beauty of the spot. Suddenly we were greeted with an orchestration. The white-eyed vireo burst into song. A cardinal, a wren, and a nuthatch followed suit. The wood thrush chimed in. A mockingbird intruded, boisterous and aggressive, as if to break up the song fest. Then all was suddenly quiet as a sharp-shinned hawk skimmed the treetops.

Lance and Don Correll went into the baygall to gather an unusual water plant—*Hottonia inflata* (member of the Primula family and sometimes known as featherfoil or water violet)—whose roots scrape the bottom and whose tuberlike tops are inflated and float erect.

On the edge of this baygall was a toothache tree (*Xanthoxylum clava-herculis*) and known as Hercules club or prickly ash, whose cousin (*X. fagara*) grows in bushy form in Central Texas. The one we saw this day was perhaps 15 feet high with wartlike lumps on its bark. The inner wood of these welts deadens the mouth tissues; and it seemed especially powerful this spring, as the sap was running strong.

We scouted the edge of this baygall and all was desolation. Roads practically encircled it. Summer houses were going up; subdivision signs were on display. Heroic efforts would be needed to save even this 20-acre tract, for, as we left, we heard of plans to turn it into a cow and horse pasture.

We went to the corner of Liberty, Polk, and Hardin counties, walking from the narrow dirt road, where we left the jeep, a short distance through a stand of loblolly pine. The soil was a sandy loam. The trees were tall and stately, showing no limbs for 50 feet or more. A few red maple were present but the forest was essentially pine. A light wind was blowing and when we stopped to examine shelf mushrooms on a tree, the music of the treetops picked up. It never reached the crescendo I was to hear in conifer stands of far-off West Texas. But it was a soft, barely audible orchestration of strings that would put a man to sleep.

Lance and I talked about back-packing this country. "Too hot in July," he said. "But in the fall, winter, and spring it's the only way to see the Big Thicket."

Most shelf mushrooms of the Big Thicket are edible; and the one we examined was, according to Lance, particularly juicy. "More protein in a pound than beef," he commented.

Larry Walker joined us to say that at this elevation—which was perhaps a dozen feet above the bottom lands—there would be an oak-hickory climax forest. That is to say, if it were left undisturbed it would, over the years, be dominantly oak and hickory. Lance agreed, but added, "Trouble is, man disturbs it by cutting. Even without cutting, it is disturbed."

"How?"

"Mostly fire. And when the fires come and destroy the hardwoods, pine comes in. Some pine are indeed fire-resistant and survive."

"Then the oak-hickory climax forest is largely theory?"

Lance and Larry nodded.

We came to this area not to see the pine but an ancient magnolia that stands perhaps a dozen feet from the point where the three counties meet. It was a grand tree maybe 1,000 years old. But it had become newsworthy, not for its age and beauty, but because of the manner of its destruction. Magnolia, the first flowering tree each spring in Washington, D.C., has become associated in my mind wholly with aesthetic values. In Texas I learned that magnolia was valued as lumber for flooring and for paneling. On my visit to the Big Thicket, however, I saw it cut by the small sawmills for railroad ties. The Santa Fe that crosses the Big Thicket uses it extensively for that purpose. My heart sank as I saw the huge piles of ties piled near the Santa Fe and manufactured out of magnolia. But I was not prepared for what Lance showed me at the point where the three counties come together. In 1965 this 1,000-year-old magnolia was thriving. By April, 1966, it was dead. Lance showed me the five holes that had been bored into the base of the tree.

"Why?"

"To poison it."

"With what?"

"Arsenate of lead."

"Who did it?"

"No one knows. A fellow like the one that killed President Kennedy."

"Why was this tree on the assassin's list?"

"Some of us want the Big Thicket made a national park. Others are opposed. The opposition is trying to make the area as unattractive as possible. That's why they poisoned the big magnolia."

"Vandalism?" I said

"You haven't seen anything yet," Lance volunteered.

On the road to Fugah I saw what he meant. We traveled a dirt road, called a "push road."

"A bulldozer in one trip can push it into place," Lance explained. "That's why it's a push road."

On the road's edge dozens of magnolia lay freshly cut. They were magnificent specimens from 18 inches to 30 inches through. They were not cut for flooring, for paneling, or for railroad ties. They were cut for sheer destruction and the trunks lay rotting.

"Why?"

"To make the forest less attractive for a park."

"Did the lumber company do it?"

"No one knows. They are on its land but vandals might have done it."

Lance told me about the pitcher plants of the Big Thicket. I had first seen them in marshy spots in Maine in the 1930s. But Maine's species (*Sarracenia purpurea*) is not the Big Thicket's. The one that grows selectively in the Big Thicket is S. *alata*. It usually grows where the water visibly seeps from the ground. But Lance showed me well-drained slopes that produce pitcher plants. But on examination the subsoil was always quite moist. The plant has a yellowish bloom and stands about 18 inches

high. The insects are caught in a tubelike stalk covered at the
top by a sturdy petal. Lance opened stalk after stalk to show me
hundreds of insects being digested by the plant at the bottom of
these hollow stalks. He and Don Correll also showed me the
Drosera, or sundew, of which there are four species in the Big
Thicket. It was in a way more interesting, as I had never seen
it before. It's a small plant whose spokelike stems about two
inches long lie flat on the ground. The white flowers are tipped
with scarlet. It takes a magnifying glass to see the small leaves
which quickly wrap themselves around any insect that lands on
them.

Lance took me to a bayou to show me the bladderwort (*Utri-
cularia inflata*). Five leaves lie flat on the water, holding up the
plant that has a tall stalk. The interesting part is underwater,
where the roots spread out like a seine. The roots are covered
with traps. When an insect touches a trap, it opens and holds
the intruder until digestion is completed. Then the trap opens
and the parts not wanted are discarded. Lance explained that
the Big Thicket has eight species of bladderwort, one of which,

working the same way, catches insects in mud rather than in water.

Still another carnivorous plant grows in the Big Thicket—the bog violet or butterwort (*Pinguicula pumila*), which we looked for but did not find.

Menard Creek, tributary of the Trinity, runs for many miles in a winding course across the Big Thicket. I had thought of the Big Thicket as very marshy with brackish bayous. There are bay-galls and bayous but they are small and composed of fresh water. The country served by Menard Creek is well drained. Lance took me down a stretch of it. We had seen hundreds of dogwood in bloom throughout the Big Thicket and were to reach Wood-ville on the northern edge just as its annual Dogwood Festival ended. Woodville has what purports to be the largest dogwood tree in the world. On Menard Creek we saw no champions, though each specimen was bright and gay.

"It's actually a melancholy tree," Lance explained. "Folklore is that the cross on which Jesus died was dogwood." Picking a broad white flower, he pointed to four rusty spots on each petal. "Those mark the places where the nails were driven through his hands and feet."

The following legend of the dogwood is told in the Big Thicket:

At the time of the Crucifixion the dogwood attained the size of the oak and other forest trees. The wood was so strong and firm that is was chosen for the timber of the Cross. To be thus used for such a purpose distressed the tree, and Jesus smiled upon it, sensed this, and, in His gentle pity for sorrow, said to it:

"Because of your regret and pity for my suffering, I make you this promise: Never again shall the dogwood tree grow big enough to be used for a cross. Henceforth it shall be slender and bent and twisted, and its blossoms shall be in the form of a cross— two long petals and two short petals—and in the center of the outer edge of each petal there will be nail prints, brown with rust and stained with blood. And in the center of the flower there shall be an image of the crown of thorns, and all who see it will remember that is was upon a dogwood tree that I was crucified, and this tree shall not be mutilated or destroyed, but cherished as a reminder of my death upon the cross."

We saw the redbud (or Judas tree), so named because folklore has it that Judas hanged himself from a branch of the Asiatic species. Its petals seem to come not from a twig but out of the bark itself. "You see the tree bleeds because of Judas' treachery."

The dogwood and redbud made even cutover land seem gay and joyous. But the rhododendrons and azaleas we saw were the most striking of all. The order of flowering for the shrubs of the Big Thicket is as follows: cross vine, yellow jasmine, hawthorn (of which there are 20 species), azalea and rhododendron, wisteria, dogwood, and smoke tree. All but the smoke tree was in display when we hiked Menard Creek. And the showiest were the azaleas that sometimes stood so thick that they looked like a planted hedge. The flower that caught my eye was a huge pink one as large as the orchid one buys at the florist for his lady.

Lance produced a low blueberry in bloom that fruits in early summer and is much prized in the kitchen. He also showed me a tree type of blueberry that fruits in the fall and furnishes much feed for the birds. He found a small specimen of poison sumac that grows up to 25 feet high, a shrub more poisonous than poison ivy or poison oak.

"But it is useful to man," he added. "The sap is used to make varnish. It is also useful to animals. Fifteen species of birds and the cottontail rabbit feed on it."

We came across a Texas buckeye, a shrub about eight feet high whose scarlet flowers were freshly in bloom—a relative of the whitebark Ohio buckeye, on whose mast the now-extinct carrier pigeon was largely dependent.

A few huge cypress—more than two feet in diameter and prob-

ably 200 years old—had somehow escaped the lumber operations that had ravaged Menard Creek and stood in splendor in
damp places. We stopped to make a boring on a loblolly pine;
it had a diameter of 14 inches and was thirty-two years old.

"It's now big enough to be commercial," Lance volunteered.

We came across river birch (*Betula nigra*), the same species
that we have in the Potomac Valley and the only native birch
in Texas—semi-aquatic, tall, with dull red-brown bark peeling
off in thin, curly flakes.

Menard Creek boasts a few American beech, which to my
eye was the same as the beech of New Hampshire, though some
botanists claim the beech of East Texas has minor variations and
dub it a Carolina beech. It was like meeting an old, old friend
and I walked up to it and put my hand on its light-gray, smooth
bark, and caressed it fondly. Nearby was a 20-foot ironwood tree
(hop hornbeam) more than 12 inches in diameter, a tree sometimes used for fence posts. A huge American sweet gum—80 feet
or more high—was also in this alcove along Menard Creek. Closer
to the water grew a huge water tupelo (*Nyssa aquatica*). Black-
berries were thick in the open places, being very showy now
that their blossoms were out. Lance stooped to show me the
dewberry trailing and tough and almost ready to bloom.

"People of the Big Thicket like its berries best of all for jelly."

A sow cleared the creek easily but her little ones in panic
struggled to get across.

We stopped our hike down Menard Creek at the point where
Meeting House Creek comes in. The two form an irregular-
shaped pool at this spot, perhaps 100 by 50 feet and 6 or more
feet deep. It is known as Barrett Swimming Hole and is famous
in Big Thicket history.

A white-eyed vireo was singing. A belted woodpecker streaked
across treetops. Somewhere in the distance a pileated woodpecker
was hammering in a hardwood.

"Know what the people of the Big Thicket call him?" Lance asked. "He's known as Lord God, he's so big and startling."

There was a splash in the pool that sounded like muskrat to me. "No, it's a nutria," Lance explained. It's the size of a coon with a tail like a possum.

"Fur is valuable and people eat it," Lance said. "And it can whip even a big dog, grabbing it by the nose and dragging it under."

We sat in silence, drinking in the beauties of the swimming hole. A frog started croaking. Eight species of tree frogs are found in the Big Thicket. Man's interest, however, is mainly in the bullfrog. "Frogs are mostly gone," Lance said. "Commercial poachers have got most of them."

Dempsie Henley spoke up to say that the fish in the Big Thicket were also disappearing. "The poachers use an old telephone with batteries and put the live wire into the water and crank the handle vigorously, which causes a shock to go into the water and momentarily paralyzes the fish. They come to the surface and then are picked up and usually sold throughout the area. Efforts are under way to prohibit such activities; however, to my knowledge, these unsportsmanlike activities continue to this hour."

Bear, beaver, and panther, once numerous, are now practically extinct.

Menard Creek has cool, clear, spring-fed waters. Barrett Swimming Hole, as a sanctuary, rates with any that I know in all of Appalachia. Yet it is on the verge of destruction. Every day 50 acres of the Big Thicket are devoured. Men are converting every acre into dollars, although its greater values are spiritual and aesthetic.

Land that in 1960 sold for $50 an acre was selling for $300 in 1966. Big development programs, in the form of subdivisions composed of small lots, are spreading everywhere. They and the

ruthless cutting programs of lumber companies are appropriating the modern Naboth's Vineyard to an end that these wondrous pieces of God's creation do not deserve.

One part of the Big Thicket looks like a pine plantation. It
is the area known as Kaiser's Burn Out. Jim Kaiser was an officer
in the Confederate Army and went in search of Texans who
avoided military service for the South by hiding in the Big
Thicket. Over and again Kaiser sent troops combing the "tight
eye" woods for the Jayhawks. But the latter were wily and re-
sourceful and knew the Big Thicket better than did the soldiers.
They easily eluded their hunters and few if any were apprehended.
But the Jayhawks, numbering about 100, needed some staples in
order to survive. So they maintained lines of communication
with the settlements. They collected honey and left it at a desig-
nated spot—now known as Honey Island—where village women
came to get it, leaving staples in return. (In the Big Thicket any
site agreed on for a meeting point or depository is an "island.")
They dressed hides for money with which to buy ammunition,
coffee, and molasses. Tobacco was pressed in the heart of a tree,
a block of a large tree being cut from one side and removed,
the tobacco leaves inserted, and the slice of wood replaced and
held by a tight tourniquet. Tobacco leaves mixed with molasses
and so pressed made good Big Thicket chewing tobacco. The
Jayhawks raised some corn and potatoes and kept a few cows.
They made whiskey out of the corn that they grew and that
their friends smuggled to them and traded wild honey for coffee.
They trapped, fished, and hunted. There were plenty of deer
then, as well as turkey and squirrel.

Some say that Kaiser courted a girl whose brother was a Jay-
hawk and she told Kaiser where they were. Others say a man
named Lilly played the role of Judas—a man who was shot by
the Jayhawks "in the fork of his galluses." Whatever may be
the truth, Kaiser waited until the wind was right and then started

a forest fire that roared toward the target. The Jayhawks escaped and are the great-grandfathers of many present-day Thicketeers. But the Kaiser Burn Out scorched the land so thoroughly that for more than 60 years nothing would grow. Finally, about 1930, a lumber company planted it in pine, and the planting was so orderly that today the area looks like a manicured park or plantation.

Near Saratoga is Pine Island Bayou, a 4,000-acre tract that has been largely untouched except for grazing by cattle. It is unique in that its dominant plant is the bush palmetto (*Sabal minor*), mostly shrublike but at times shaping up into a 25-foot tree. This palmetto appears throughout the Big Thicket. In this particular area it is thick, making up the dominant tree. The flowers are a source of honey; tannic acid is extracted from the stalks; and the berries, when crushed, produce a juice used by the Indians to relieve the pressure of an enlarged prostate.

Several species of hawthorn were mixed with the palmettos and they were in bloom. The honey locust, whose pods are relished by cattle, deer, squirrels, and rabbits, was common. Many species of oak were present but hardly any pine. An occasional cypress of gargantuan proportions touched the sky. But the rest, including the palmettos, hawthorn, and honey locust, made up a thick understory. The common persimmon was present. Cedar elm, that sometimes reaches 90 feet, was a short, stiff-branched tree in this bayou. The water elm (*Planera aquatica*) was also present—a clean tree that likes to have its feet in water. Indians used its wood for making spoons.

Here was the American cyrilla or leatherwood, its small, white, fragrant flowers very much on display.

Many of these trees had ferns growing in their crotches and along some limbs. They had gone unnoticed until Don Correll pointed them out.

"They turn green when it rains," Don said. "Transforms a

whole forest." They are the resurrection fern (*Polypodium poly-podioides*) that we find in Maryland.

All the trees in this bayou area were heavy with Spanish moss, and at one stop Lance held forth on mosses. He talked first about the Spanish moss and told the legend of its origin—how the North Wind fought the South Wind, the latter winning. And when South won, it tore the beard off North, scattering it far and wide.

"That's how we got Spanish moss."

Lance also talked of other mosses that grow on tree trunks.

"Up North the moss may grow only on the north side of a tree. I've heard tell that's true in Maine. Not so down here. You can't count on finding your direction from the moss."

By the roadside where we left this bayou were bright blue streaks of verbena and less conspicuous clumps of a delicate blue-eyed grass.

"Here's something special I want to show you," said Lance as he dropped to his knees. He pointed to a procumbent herb-like plant with small, solitary, tubelike blue flowers—a plant so inconspicuous that the average passer-by would miss it entirely.

"This is *Anagallis arvensis*," Lance said. "Known as the poor-man's-weather-glass." He went on to explain that the flowers opened only on clear days, quickly closing at the approach of bad weather.

Don Correll took pains to point out that some of the flora of Appalachia is in the Big Thicket, the flowers coming in a direct line from Tennessee, across northern Alabama and northern Mississippi through Arkansas into East Texas. The list is long. In that manner came species of the grass-of-Parnassus, the tooth-wort, holly, alum root, the milkweed, the nodding pogonia, magnolia, and rhododendron. He explained that, as each species reaches its western extremes in East Texas, it has a tendency to differ in some degree from plants of the same species found farther east. "The variations are often so great," he said, "that the plant has to be segregated as a distinct species."

That is why the Big Thicket is called "a region of specia-tion" by the botanists and one reason why it is so highly valued by them. Another reason is that the area is rich in fungi, at least 1,000 species of which have never been classified.

In the northwestern part of the Big Thicket, between Living-ston and Woodville and near Highway 190, is the Alabama–Coushatta Indian Reservation of some 4,300 acres, two-thirds of which was purchased by the Federal government, the rest being purchased by Texas. The Federal government later relinquished its trusteeship of the lands and Texas took over. Texas supplies a superintendent; and Dempsie Henley is Commissioner of Indian Affairs. Two tribal chiefs—B. Cooper Sylestine and Fulton Battise —and a tribal council govern the two tribes; and they made me an Honorary Life Time Member in a ceremony which included the performance of many Indian dances.

The Coushattas came to Texas from Tennessee about 1795, while the Alabamas, traveling through several Southern states, reached Texas in 1816. They always had peaceful relations with the other settlers and Sam Houston tried desperately to be-friend them.

In the early days a settler, anxious to learn how they settled disputes among themselves, asked one Indian, "Suppose Charlie Thompson had a bad horse and you had a bad fence and Charlie's horse gets in your field and destroys some of your corn and you want him to pay you for your corn?"

The Indian answered by saying, "Charlie got no bad horse; me no bad fence."

The settler then asked, "Suppose your hogs and Charlie's hogs run in the bottom together and your hogs look so much like his hogs that Charlie claims all of the hogs?"

The Indian answered, "Me know my hogs; Charlie knows his hogs."

"Suppose he does not know his hogs and claims yours?"

The Indian replied, "I give Charlie my hogs."

The reservation now has 360 inhabitants, all full-blooded, all devout Christians, mostly Presbyterians.

The reservation offers employment for only ten residents; the others must find employment in nearby towns. Dempsie Henley, the Texas commissioner who supervises them, and Price Daniel, their dollar-a-year lawyer, are turning their attention to tourism. Education in handicrafts is being promoted and some of the lost Indian arts are being restored. Girls and women now weave attractive rugs for sale at the reservation headquarters. They also make beautiful baskets out of the longleaf needles of yellow pine. Moreover, an outdoor theater with a stage has been built where the Indians put on tribal dances for visitors, as many as 2,000 tourists showing up on weekends for the performance.

They also have open busses with a four-wheel drive that take visitors on hour-long tours of a primitive forest. The forest, which contains about 300 acres, is indeed primitive, one of the few places in the Big Thicket that can be accurately described as such. On this tour one can see an open-type forest, as distinguished from a "tight eye." Gums and cypress are there. The shagbark hickory and white ash are seen. Lots of patrician beech are on display. Magnificent ironwood are there, a tree, according to one of the chiefs, that was considered a choice wood for the making of bows. But the dominant tree is the loblolly pine. One loblolly stood with another of equal size but it became necessary to cut the latter. Its cross section, now in the museum on the reservation, shows "good" and "dry" years dating back to 1772.

"Anything like your redwoods?" Lance asked.

"It is getting into their class," I replied.

This virgin forest is on rolling red clay land, perhaps 300 feet above sea level. Its open effect brings lots of sunshine to the forest floor; and when I was there the whole floor litter had a yellowish cast from the host of buttercups that were at their peak.

We left the reservation at dusk to the music of the whippoor-wills.

Pipe lines without rhyme or reason have cut the Big Thicket into many pieces, condemning private lands willy-nilly with no power on the part of a state officer or of citizens to stop them.

Oil companies have ruined hundreds of acres by allowing salt water from their wells to flood the land. We stopped at one such place where Lance sadly reported, as though speaking at an inquest;

"Here used to be the finest stand of the pitcher plant in all the Big Thicket. Now nothing will grow."

There are many species of birds in the Big Thicket, at least 300 in number. These include the cattle egret, a bird that in recent decades crossed the Atlantic from North Africa and came to us via Latin America. The legs and bill are yellow, the body white. It's a small-chicken-sized bird. It eats only insects and follows cattle because their movements stir up insects from the grass. In the Big Thicket I saw some of these birds sitting on the backs of cattle picking off lice and mosquitoes.

The anhinga or water turkey is found in the Big Thicket. It is three feet high and has a four-foot wingspread. Its neck is long and slender, its bill slim and straight. The male is greenish-black; the female's head, neck, and breast are grayish-buff. It uses its bill to spear fish on which it feeds exclusively. It swims under-water in pursuit of its prey and when it begins to surface, its tail comes up in the shape of a disk, like a turkey's. It has little oil on its wings and body. So, after swimming, it cannot fly for a while. Thus, it spends hours each day drying its feathers on the sunny side of a tree.

The spoonbill is in the Big Thicket. It stands about 30 inches high and has a wingspread of four feet. It has a yellowish-green head, a white breast and back, and a pale rose-pink body with splashes of crimson over the tail and shoulders. Its long, greenish bill is flattened like a spatula. It feeds as it wades, living mostly on crustaceans and minnows.

The great American egret is in the Big Thicket. It has a yellow bill and black legs and is entirely white, standing about three feet high. During breeding season it grows long, streaming plumes on its back—plumes that once were greatly sought for ladies' hats; as a result of which the birds, by the turn of this century, became practically extinct. But, thanks to the Audubon Society, they were saved.

The great blue heron, often called a crane by the country

people, is in the Big Thicket. It stands four feet high and, next to the sandhill crane, is the largest wading bird in the States. It went out ahead of us on bayous calling hoarsely, *frahnk, frahnk.*

The great white heron is in the Big Thicket—pure white with yellow beak and greenish-yellow legs. By 1935 it was close to extinction.

These great birds came into our conversation as we got glimpses of them, some at a considerable distance, when we stopped to look at a half section that was blighted and blistered.

"Planes sprayed the hardwoods," Lance explained.

"Why?"

"To kill them so that pine would grow. You see, pine grows faster and makes more money for the lumber companies."

"Any side effects?" I asked.

Lance choked up with emotion, saying:

"This was a rookery that they sprayed at a time when hundreds of big birds were nesting—herons, American egrets, spoonbills, and anhingas."

"What happened?"

"All the birds were killed except seven. Counted them myself. Dozens of young ones lay in their nests, their heads hanging over the side. Worst vandalism I ever knew."

We saw other tracts similarly sprayed that were now patches of desolation.

The ivory-billed woodpecker is in the Big Thicket. It is larger than a crow, the male having a flaming red crest, the female a black one. It has an ivory-white bill and large white wing patches visible when the bird is at rest. It is close to extinction; but Lance knows where it lives in the Big Thicket. This woodpecker needs the dead or dying logs of a wild virgin area for nesting purposes, and for grubs and other insects on which it feeds. It has difficulty surviving where the forests are cleaned out.

Lance offered to take me to them.

"I usually don't do it," he said, "because once the word gets around, the poachers move in. When a species is near extinction, one bird becomes quite a trophy."

I declined the invitation with thanks, thinking that perhaps man's greatest contribution was to stay away from their environment, leaving them alone and introducing no element of anxiety.

But the Big Thicket is an anxiety breeding area. The environment perpetuates the poacher's tradition. In the nineteenth century man hunted for the joy of it. Judge Hightower, already mentioned, is reputed to have killed more than 200 bears in the Big Thicket, one with a bowie knife, and as many as four a day. Another hunter was Bud Bracken of Kountze, who has the record of killing 305 bears. He hunted with dogs, and once, when a huge bear charged, he ran out of ammunition and ended up using the gun as a club and running the barrel down the bear's throat with the result that the barrel was dented and would not shoot straight any more.

What grandfather did, grandson does today. The fox squirrels that are found on the ridges and the gray squirrels that frequent the bottom lands make for more popular hunting than does the Virginia deer. The Thicketeers hunt for hunting's sake. No game laws were indeed sought to be enforced until 1964. The wardens' jobs are, as I have said, not only onerous but truly dangerous. A vast educational program is needed to convert the Thicketeers to the cause of conservation.

The plight of the bald eagle is a case in point. This species has been greatly depleted due to the extensive use of DDT that gets into the water and eventually into the fish that the bald eagle eats. DDT, not being soluble, is stored in the body; and birds, including the bald eagle, are very susceptible to it. Poachers have decimated what remains of them in the Big Thicket.

"Only four remain where there once were hundreds," Lance said. "Poachers mainly responsible."

Congress, in the Wilderness Act of 1964, 78 Stat. 890, defined "wilderness" for the purpose of the Act as follows:

> A wilderness, in contrast with those areas where man and his own works dominate the landscape, is hereby recognized as an area where the earth and its community of life are untrammeled by man, where man himself is a visitor who does not remain. An area of wilderness is further defined to mean in this Act an area of undeveloped Federal land retaining its primeval character and influence, without permanent improvements or human habitation, which is protected and managed so as to preserve its natural conditions and which (1) generally appears to have been affected primarily by the forces of nature, with the imprint of man's work substantially unnoticeable; (2) has outstanding opportunities for solitude or a primitive and unconfined type of recreation; (3) has at least five thousand acres of land or is of sufficient size as to make practicable its preservation and use in an unimpaired condition; and (4) may also contain ecological, geological, or other features of scientific, educational, scenic, or historical value.

There are parts of the Big Thicket that meet most of those requirements; but no part of it embraces 5,000 acres. Untouched primitive areas of the kind described by Congress do exist, such as the 20-acre baygall I described, the 300-acre unit in the Indian Reservation, and other tracts of various sizes, all short of 5,000 acres. So it is not possible to fit the Big Thicket into the concept of a "wilderness" area.

The alternatives in terms of existing categories are either a state park or a national park. The logging companies and the other interests opposed are solidly for a state park, if any change in the *status quo* is to be made. By relegating the promotion of this project into state channels, they feel confident they can defeat it. For the state government is solidly controlled by The Establishment.

Conservationists know that their only hope is in Federal action. And the Big Thicket Association, that now has more than 5,000 members, is working diligently toward that objective. Yet, even by Federal standards there are difficulties. The Big Thicket is so badly chewed up by civilization that there is no one vast unit that can be set aside comparable in dignity to our other national parks. What remain are islands of beauty and wilderness—what Dempsie Henley calls a "string of pearls"—a baygall here, a bayou there, 500 or 1,000 acres on Menard Creek, the Kaiser Burn Out, the Pine Island Bayou stand of bush palmetto, and the like.

The Big Thicket Association, headed by Dempsie Henley and Lance Rosier, has been feverishly attempting to raise money to buy choice tracts that are headed for decimation by lumber firms and pulpwood users. One man, Raymond H. McDavid, put up $10,000 of his own money to keep an option on a choice plot while the search for public funds got under way.

Public interest mounts and public enthusiasm increases. But the race will be a close one, as the modern Ahabs are strong, well-financed, and influential.

One large tract is needed where in time the original Big Thicket would come back by natural regeneration. Smaller tracts would illustrate the different vegetational types. There are, moreover, sites where important events took place that are interesting chapters in American history: a typical pioneer farm carved out of the forest, an early sawmill, a ghost town, and the like.

A mill town such as Silsbee could develop an interesting museum around Julian Henry Kirby, his life, and the works of Kirby Lumber Company. John Henry Kirby came to the Big Thicket in 1884. He was an imposing man in appearance. One day he was getting a shoeshine when one passer-by asked another who that man was.

"That's John Henry Kirby."

"Who's Kirby?"

"John Henry Kirby? Why, in East Texas the sun doesn't rise until John Henry Kirby crows."

Some think a scenic parkway should link all these "pearls." Others are opposed, saying that existing roads are adequate, that a new scenic parkway would be destructive of the precious little bits of wilderness that remain.

The basic plan for a national park is sound. But it takes on the average from six to eight years to get a bill through the Congress, establishing a national park. We are losing 50 acres a day, as I have said. At that rate the Big Thicket will be down to less than 200,000 acres in six years and to about 140,000 in eight years.

Time is on the side of the modern Ahabs, not on the side of the people.

They have allies in Washington, D.C., as well as in Texas. While the plans for a national park get under way, the Southeast Texas Resource Conservation and Development group, working with the Soil Conservation Service of the Federal government, has drainage plans for all the counties of the Big Thicket that would open up many acres for rice farming and other commercial projects. Those plans would drastically affect and change the ecology, flora, and fauna of the entire area and completely destroy the Big Thicket.

But the hopes of the conservationists still ride high. For on October 20, 1966 Senator Ralph Yarborough of Texas introduced a bill to make the Big Thicket a national park. It is around that measure that everyone in the fifty states who loves the wilderness and the outdoors will rally. For the Big Thicket is so unique and so lovely that it should belong to *all* the people.

CHAPTER II

THE BIG BEND

The Big Bend country in West Texas, once cruelly treated by stockmen through overgrazing, faced a like fate. The Big Bend is an oblong stretch of dry, empty West Texas land, brown for most of the year, that is bounded by the Pecos River on the east, the Rio Grande on the south and west, and New Mexico on the north. It has rolling plains, but also lofty mountains and deep, yawning canyons. Seven hundred thousand-odd acres in the south central part of this Big Bend country are now in the Big Bend National Park.

This park was the product of a combination of two forces: first, the people of Alpine, Marfa, and Marathon who were hungry for the tourist business, and second, the submarginal—or as one rancher put it, "the sub-submarginal"—cattlemen who wanted to sell out to the government after they had ruined the land.

There were many people in the end responsible for the park. But E. E. Townsend was rightfully the father who, beginning in 1933, promoted the project in the Texas legislature. That year the Texas legislature started acquiring land for Big Bend State Park. In 1935 the National Park Service became interested and had surveys made. The project gained momentum; the Texas legislative appropriations and private subscriptions resulted in more than 690,000 acres being acquired; and a Federal Act was passed (49 Stat. 393) looking to the receipt of those lands from the state and the creation of a Federal park. The Governor of Texas, Coke R. Stevenson, presented the deed to the parklands to a Federal agent in Alpine on September 5, 1943. On February 12, 1944, he presented to Amon A. Carter the deed of cession, conveying jurisdiction over the Big Bend National Park from the state of Texas to the United States with a request that Carter deliver the instrument to President Roosevelt. That was done on June 6, 1944, and on June 12, 1944, the Big Bend National Park —708,000 acres all in Brewster County—was officially established. The National Park Service took over administration on July 5, 1944.

The best distant view of Big Bend is from the highway, Route 67, between Presidio and Marfa, where it crosses a height of land known as Frenchman's Hill. On the left or north are the Davis Mountains, and on the right or south are the Chisos. Both are so far away that they have a purplish cast. The Rio Grande that cuts its way south of the Chisos is out of view. The land between the two ranges is vast, rolling, and seemingly empty. It is cut up by arroyos and dotted with buttes and mesas. There is no sign of habitation; no touch of green (except after a rain)— only somber grays and browns.

Mount Livermore (8,382 feet), the second highest in Texas (named for Captain W. R. Livermore, who surveyed the Big Bend in 1884), looms in the north and Mount Emory (7,835 feet), third highest in Texas, marks the Chisos in the south.

This is bleak, wasted land stretching as far as one can see. One day, as we stood in wonder on Frenchman's Hill, Jim Bowmer recited an old Texas ballad:

> No water, no shade, and the glare's a sin,
> So dry, I'm spittin' cotton, I'm all done in!
> I swanee, I never have felt such heat!

No tank in sight for my burning feet.
A little piece down this dusty road,
There lay a plumb dried-up horny toad!
The fence-posts seen set antigodlin' . . .
Or is it me, that's reeling . . . toddlin'?

Cheer my way with a song
I must mosey along . . .
Kick up hot West-Texas sand
Till I get to the hide-out land
'Cross the good, old Rio Grande,
Good, old Rio Grande . . .

Two main roads enter the park on the north: No. 385 from
Marathon, 39 miles distant, and No. 118 from Alpine, 81 miles
distant. These two roads converge at Panther Junction where
park headquarters are located. West of that point by about three
miles is a road to the south that leads in seven miles to Chisos
Basin, where there are camping facilities, motels, a restaurant,
post office, souvenir shop, and riding stables. Beyond Panther
Junction to the east is a road to a campground at Rio Grande
Village on the Rio Grande just above the entrance to Boquillas
Canyon and just across from the Mexican village of Boquillas.

The entrance road down from Marathon passes close to Dagger
Flat where a forest of giant yuccas, gay with whitish flowers,
transforms the desert of the Southwest. While the Mojave is
noted for its Joshua tree yucca, and the Sonora for the giant
saguaro cactus, the Chihuahua, out of which the Big Bend rises,
is marked not only by the giant dagger yucca but the lechuguilla as well, whose green, bananalike leaves are so thorny
that goats will not touch them. The bottom lands are dotted
with cactus—some 40 varieties—and they bloom not all at once
but in sequence, painting streaks of pink, yellow, purple, red,
and white across a brownish, seared land. The graceful ocotillo

sends out bright green leaves following a rain even in winter, and when its red flowers are out, these plants look like desert flagpoles. Greasewood, buckthorn, soapberry, Mexican buckeye, and cenisa dot the desert; and an occasional mesquite, with a vast underground network of roots, stands in splendor.

Eons ago—in what geologists call the Cretaceous period (65 million years ago)—this area was under the sea; and that period produced chalk, sandstone, shale, conglomerate, and limestone. Some of these were laid down in layers several thousand feet thick which uplift and erosion have put on display. The ancient sea that overlay the area apparently oscillated back and forth, and in the interim produced broad, flat river plains, for remnants of palms, fish scales, bones of turtles, crocodiles, marine reptiles and dinosaurs, and shark and ray teeth are found in the sedimentary rocks. There must have been a rather thick cover of vegetation, as some coal is found. These sedimentary rocks at close range and at a distance are bright and gay, their reds resplendent in the lowering sun, their yellows bright at midday.

From 5 to 20 million years ago in the Tertiary period and after the great uplift of the sedimentary rocks came other sandstones and clays that today yield vertebrate fossils. This was the time when mammals replaced the dinosaurs. The hydracotherium—an animal not much larger than a fox, but probably a direct ancestor of the horse—is one of these mammals; and the skeleton of one is on display at a Fossil Site on Tornillo Creek off Route 385 within the park.

This geological potpourri makes the Big Bend a happy hunting ground for geologists. For the layman it offers exciting diversity in formations, in color, and in vistas. There are painted skylines, painted cliffs, painted alcoves. This desert country that makes up the lower reaches of the park is an excellent winter hiking area. Odd rock formations add a touch of mystery. And he who is in earnest can find outcroppings of flint and nodules of agate that the Indians used to make arrowhead and dart points, one of the most famous being Burro Mesa.

Lava followed the sandstones and clay. The lava was in turn invaded by intrusive rocks—granite, feldspar, and biotite.

One who takes the twenty-mile auto trip from park headquarters to Boquillas finds spacious campgrounds, peculiarly attractive for wintertime use. This is known as the Rio Grande Village area, fed by two springs from an old farm, springs that produce about 65 gallons a minute. The Park Service has put the two farms together, installed a pumping station, irrigated a goodly bit of the river bottom, planted cottonwood and mesquite, and installed drinking fountains, rest rooms, and cooking facilities in the form of metal braziers standing on stems about waist high. This brazier is used in lieu of the fireplace, because wood is scarce, charcoal and briquets being burned instead. Some family campsites have a roof without sidewalls—a *ramada* —that provides some shade. There are, of course, alcoves for trailers—and picnic tables. These Rio Grande campgrounds are extensively used in the winter. And though the temperatures reach 115° in the summer, a surprising number of people use them then. Attractive river pools invite swimming, and low humidity makes the shade of mesquite especially appealing.

In this Rio Grande Village area is a warm-water pond constructed by the Park Service to sustain a rare species of fish— the *Gambusia gargei*. Another species thrives in the Everglades, feeding on mosquito larvae and starting a food chain that ends with the alligator. The Rio Grande *Gambusia* claims no such distinction. But it is a tiny warm-water minnow recently discovered and thriving in Park waters.

I have stood on a height of land in the Chihuahua Desert watching all points of the compass for hours on end and not seen any sign of life. There is, however, much game in the desert wilderness. In the lower reaches are the large desert mule or blacktail deer, weighing around 200 pounds, and ranchers are beginning to treat them as a cash crop. Some give access to their lands at $15 a day, the hunter providing food, shelter, and transportation. Some charge $300 for a ten-day period, supplying lodging and food and jeep transport. They even go so far as to allot territory to hunters. The income of some ranchers from these hunting privileges exceeds $20,000 a year. "It makes the cattle business worth while," one rawboned cattleman told me.

Higher up are the Sonora fantail deer, that run about 70 pounds. Javelina or collared peccary are in the hills. These are animals fairly easy to approach and relatively safe, except when dogs are around. They do tree a man with dogs and they fight the canine, moving their tusks in a flat plane back and forth. But they are not nearly so ferocious or as deadly as the European boar.

There are coyote and kit fox on the prowl. The pronghorn antelope is occasionally seen. That animal is a grassland product and Big Bend is south of the prime grasslands. Its land is partly in a desert region and partly in browse. Higher up the grass takes over. But the antelope is an animal of the plains. The antelope in Big Bend have been mostly imported from up north; and they tend to emigrate to their more natural environment. Of the 1933 pronghorns planted in the park during 1947-1948, most of them moved to grasslands in the north and outside the park. But a visitor in Big Bend sees a few, their saucy white tails flashing in the distance. An occasional black bear is found. But during the twenty years Big Bend has been a park, only one bear was reported; it was feeding on the green seed pods of century plants. That was in 1952.

At night the ringtail cat—which looks very much like a house cat—is on the prowl. The cougar and gray fox also start moving then. Road runners (*paisanos*)—a fast-running member of the cuckoo family—are common.

There are more than 30 species of snakes in Big Bend. But

most of them are non-poisonous. There are one species of copperhead and five of rattlesnakes, including the western diamondback. But they are not often seen. One who walks is always aware of their presence. But they are indeed difficult to find if one is on a search.

The rarest snake in the Big Bend country is the Davis Mountains king snake—*Lampropettis alterna*—which ranges from the Chisos to the Davis Mountain range but also is rarely seen.

The orange eyes that the headlights pick up along the road's edge are those of poorwills, cousins of nighthawks and whippoorwills.

The state of Texas has established the Black Gap Wildlife Management Area which is about 50 miles south of Marathon, bordered on the west by the Big Bend National Park and on the south by Mexico. The area now approximates 100,000 acres in

size. The native game species are desert mule deer, the blue or scaled quail, the javelina, and the antelope. Chukar partridge—the buff-colored birds with white meat that were imported from Iran—have been released in the area and they are flourishing. And the desert bighorn sheep has been placed there. This is a re-introduction, for the desert bighorn originally ranged this Big Bend country.

Much field research goes on in this management area. The desert bighorn are kept in a predator-proof 600-acre enclosure. They will be released once the holding pasture reaches full stocking capacity. This re-introduction of the desert bighorn began in 1958 when two Arizona ewes were flown to Texas and deposited in the holding pasture. Many others have been added to the herd, some dying, some thriving and reproducing.

The enclosure is located at an elevation of 2,800 feet in a limestone-type formation with a high ridge down the center. It has an abundance of vegetation and is cut up into a network of draws and small canyons. These animals have been given some supplementary feed but they have mainly survived upon the native plants, one of the favorite being lechuguilla, which they seem to consume in its entirety, including the roots. Although there are many questions still unanswered concerning the future of bighorns in Texas, the experts in game management have a hopeful outlook for their restoration.

Interesting as the Chihuahua Desert is, the main charms and attractions for me are the high ridges and basins. There man gets respite from the valley heat. There is found a complex of life that is unique in the American outdoors.

The Chisos Mountains are isolated between the southernmost spear of the Rocky Mountain system and the Sierra Madres, ranging northward from Mexico. They are in the form of a rough circle of peaks about six miles across, rising in the midst of a sloping plain surrounded by foothills.

Baja del Sol, a famous Apache chief, lived in the Chisos canyons after he had been driven by the white man from the high country. He was supposed to stay in Mexico. But according to legend he in time got homesick for the Chisos and returned there, living in caves, foraging at night, and evading the white patrols. He was, however, done in by his own people; and his murderers were haunted by the sound of his footsteps at night and, they even say, his ghost. So the Chisos—or Ghost Mountains—got their names.

That is only one of many legends. Professor Elton Miles of Sul Ross State College at Alpine has sorted them all out in Volume 38, Texas Folklore Society Publication (1958), pp. 106–122. The truth is that Chisos is probably a corruption of "Chishi," an Apache word meaning "forest dwellers." Yet, as Elton Miles reports, the word in the Big Bend area means "sinister, menacing humanlike beings, whose exact appearance, though Apachean, is unknown." And that is why the American translated Los Chisos as "the ghosts."

As one climbs the Chisos, he has startling views on all sides, especially toward Mexico. The Mexican massif is even higher and more rugged than the Chisos range. There will in time be a Mexican park, physically united with Big Bend for recreational uses; and it will open up to wide use the spectacular Sierra Madres Mountains to the south and the Sierra Fronterisa and the Sierra del Carmen to the southeast—the latter being a range bisected by the Rio Grande and known on the Texas side as the Dead Horse Mountains. The Mexican mountains are today only scenery for Big Bend visitors; but they offer scenery extraordinary. The Sierra del Carmen show crimson cliffs in a lowering sun; and the distant Sierra Fronterisa are washed by the shadows of fleecy clouds in midday and a thickening purplish cast as the day wanes.

Chisos Basin, where tourist facilities are located, is 5,400 feet above sea level. The mountains themselves are in the 7,000–8,000 foot range. The Basin is indeed a deep saucer. Casa Grande, a massive chimneylike peak of 7,300 feet in the Basin, is an intrusive sill, while opposite it and somewhat lower is Ward Mountain (7,076 feet), composed of tertiary volcanics topped on a portion of its upper slopes with uplifted limestone.

Many trails lead out of the Basin. One of the most scenic is the seven-mile trail to the South Rim, where a 1,500-foot escarpment provides a platform for scanning a vast domain of basins, rolling plains, isolated mesas, distant mountain ranges, and the blue thread of the Rio Grande.

Chisos Basin itself has distant vistas. A cleft in the escarpment that surrounds the Basin is known as The Window, looking west across hot plains to Terlingua. Changing sunlight sets the faraway mountains in different moods. But, whatever the outlook, the urge is to ride to the horizon, possess this seemingly empty land, and make it one's own. An hour at The Window on either a winter or a summer day stirs thoughts of conquest—not by force but by possession. The feelings of early cattlemen are easy to understand. The view is at least a hundred miles; and what I see there is something I feel I must embrace. It is a feeling I never get in wooded areas. But where trees are absent or skimpy and the land rolls to the horizon, the view unbroken, my possessive instincts are triggered.

All of us who tramp this land acquire what Frank X. Tolbert of the Dallas *Morning News* calls the Big Bend Fever. The late Walter Prescott Webb, author of *The Great Plains*, diagnosed the disease as "being homesick for a place that can never be your home." Frank Tolbert adds, "The only temporary treatment is to go adventuring several times a year among these mountain-desert-canyon fantasies."

Chisos Basin, of course, is wooded. Several kinds of juniper are present, including the drooping juniper. The branches of this juniper noticeably droop; and apart from Mexico, it is found only in the Chisos. There is also present the *one-seed* juniper, distinguished by a bark that separates into long, thin scales or fibers. The alligator juniper is the third juniper found here. It is unmistakably the alligator for its bark has nearly square plates like those on the skin of the animal of the same name. The Mexican piñon pines with large edible seeds—which in the 1920s I found on pushcarts in New York City—are quite abundant.

In the Basin, at elevations over a mile high, is the madrone tree, smooth, quite reddish in color, and popularly known as Naked Indian.

And there are several oaks in the area—gray, Emory, and Graves.

Cat's claw and mesquite are scattered. Everywhere are various species of cactus, also the yucca and the century plant.

Chisos Basin with its tourist facilities is green but not lush, refreshing but not fragrant. In the winter one needs a fire at night, the temperature sometimes dropping to nine degrees below zero. In summer it is a high alcove offering escape from the searing heat; and at night a cold wind almost always makes blankets necessary.

The areas above Chisos Basin are in many respects the most interesting. They are easy of access on good trails; and one of the most attractive is the Boot Canyon area about five miles up and out of Chisos Basin in a southerly direction. One who travels the trail in springtime is almost certain to see blossoms of the nine flaxes that frequent the Chisos, including the blue one (*Linum lewisii*) first brought to light by the Lewis and Clark Expedition to Oregon in 1805. The phlox is also present, not in vast mats such as we find in the Cascades of the Pacific Northwest, but in patches no bigger than a saucer. A small cactus with a reddish flower and a yellow center, called locally the claret cup, is quite profuse; and the Indian paintbrush (four species) is fairly common.

A thistlelike plant is in bloom, a member of the poppy family known as prickle poppy (*Argemone chisosensis*); and its open petals are white and bright.

Some small cherry trees with white flowers add a bit of gayety to the dry woods. So do the white of the serviceberry and the pink Texas redbud. But the shrubs are not on display as they are in Appalachia or in the Big Thicket. Yet their scarcity brings an occasional reward. Even one cherry tree or one redbud in bloom transforms an entire alcove dominated by grays, greens, and browns.

We went on a pack trip out of Chisos Basin, over the top to Boot Rock and Boot Canyon and out at Blue Creek. Buck Newsom, who has the horse concession in Chisos Basin, was in charge. We climbed slowly a few miles on a gentle trail thick with needles, the smell of conifers strong and fragrant. We crossed over a divide and looked down on Boot Rock—a spectacular column standing apart from the mountain mass and shaped like an inverted cowboy's boot. It dominates a sloping basin, near the top of which is a fire ranger's cabin. This is Boot Spring Camp, famous in botanical history, where we had lunch.

Peter Koch explained that Boot Canyon once had a bubbling spring that is now dry, even in wet weather. Its demise is due to an engineer who did not fathom the mystery of springs. Springs are fickle things. Water is sometimes impounded below a spring to form a pond. But at times the weight of the water in the pond is great enough to reverse the flow of the spring—permanently. A spring at other times owes its existence to the shape of a particular fissure. Any structural change may result in the spring going underground. That is what happened in Boot Canyon. An engineer put dynamite in the spring and blew it, causing it to disappear forever.

Tens of thousands of years ago—probably in the Pleistocene era—West Texas was a wet, humid country that produced much vegetation. That era has left a relic forest behind and it is on display at Boot Spring Camp.

Huge, healthy specimens of the Arizona cypress are rather thick, their rounded tips adding variety to the vegetation. Douglas fir is on display—not the huge fir of the Pacific but magnificent relics three feet in diameter and 80 feet high. And the ponderosa pine is there, too. Like the fir, it does not grow to gargantuan proportions. But it is large and majestic. Our Pacific ponderosa is the lumberman's favorite and affectionately called the "yellow-bellied" pine. But the ponderosa of the Chisos has less yellow in its bark and more brown. Yet it is a fitting member of the royal pine family.

Another relic of bygone days when the Chisos knew wet, humid weather is the big-tooth maple (*Acer grandidentatum*)— close relative of the famed sugar maple of the East. It also helps adorn Boot Canyon. The limber pine (*Pinus flexilis*), common in the Sierra Nevada, a heavy snowfall area, is also present. But there is little snow in the Chisos to test its tensile strength, which is tremendous.

A talus slope shows quaking aspen, and along with the aspen is the elderberry bush, likewise an alien by present environmental standards.

Some of the fir and cypress have been killed by beetles, and they stand as ghosts in the forests. Ten years ago people despaired because the cypress, fir, and pine were not producing. But the day Peter Koch, Jim Bowmer, and I hiked the basin the young growth was coming fast. Peter Koch was beaming. "Now there'll be fir and pine and cypress here another century."

The relic forest does indeed seem to have an excellent chance to survive. Pests are one risk; fires are another. Lightning fires are perhaps the greatest one; and some of the worst fires take place in basket grass (*Nolina erumpens*). This plant stands about three feet high, its coarse, flat leaves being minutely toothed along the margins. The whole leaves were used by the Indians for basketry. They have a thick oil content and, once lit, are highly volatile. Boot Spring lies at the top of a funnel. At the bottom, far down the valley, are stands of basket grass which, if ignited, would burn ferociously and might carry the fire in a tremendous updraft into the relic forest. But the chances of survival of the relic forest are good; and come another century, man and child will hopefully be able to see some of the glories of a forest that flourished when West Texas had 80 inches of rain or more a year.

The pine, the fir, the cypress, maple, and the quaking aspen show that a part of Colorado has been left in the Chisos. One who researches more closely discovers, as Peter Koch explained, that plants normally associated with country east of the 98th meridian are here in force; two grama grasses, three bluestems, the hop tree, hackberry, Mexican buckeye, sumac, white prickly poppy, nightshades, amarasith, and flycatcher. Climate changed drastically over the ages; but plants, like people, are stubborn; and they can survive and reproduce under conditions too hostile to admit them if they invaded today for the first time. The most striking example of adaptation is in the species of ferns—more than 20 being found in the park.

When we hiked Boot Spring Basin on this luncheon stop, we came across Couch's jay—more brilliant and lighter hued than our Stellar jay of the Pacific. There were small ant-eating woodpeckers almost without number; and blue quail were numerous. The blue-throated hummingbird is a summer resident, also found sometimes in southern Arizona but nowhere else.

Band-tailed pigeons, mourning doves, and white-winged doves were abundant. We heard but did not see a much rarer bird— the colima warbler. This is a small gray bird with a yellow spot near the base of its tail that nests only in the Chisos, spending its winters in Mexico. Its call, which is very much like that of the chipping sparrow, came over and again from the relic forests. When the park was being put together, a strange man, hearing that the colima warbler was almost extinct, decided he would collect the last specimens of the species. So he went into Boot Spring Basin and shot all he could find and skinned them out. Happily he missed having a collector's item, for he overlooked some colima warblers who still flourish in the Basin and on its ridges.

After lunch we climbed over the ridge above Boot Spring Basin to Laguna Meadows. Once those meadows embraced a two-acre lake. But denuding the vegetation through overgrazing caused heavy runoffs that cut through the wall of the natural reservoir, reducing the lake to a small puddle which the drought of the fifties and the lean years of the sixties dried up. These meadows, heavily pounded in the 1920s by goats and cattle, show bunch grass interspersed with barren soil that the wind has whipped ferociously. They may in time come back. But man was a predator when it came to these high meadows just as he was when he tried to collect the last specimen of the colima warbler.

Laguna has a floor made up of a volcanic intrusive. The hillsides around it are composed of badly eroded limestone. The

igneous rock has a quite different floral community than the limestone. The proximity of the two attracts botanists. Biologists and zoologists are also drawn to Laguna like a magnet. It was here that a Schmidt fence lizard was discovered—the desert side-blotched lizard (*Uta stansburiana stegnegeri Schmidt*). On Blue Creek, which drains out of Laguna, came one of the first known worm snakes—*Leptotyphlops humilis segregus*—an animal that rarely comes to the surface but lives deep in damp earth.

We were discussing these things as we rested under a piñon pine at Laguna. Peter Koch described the wonders of the Chisos and blessed the park that brought protection to these high, dry lands. Pointing to a talus slope off to the east on the slopes of Mount Emory, he talked about another small relic forest—aspen quaking in the wind—aspen that are as healthy as any in Colorado. Buck Newsom interrupted to call our attention to a stinger scorpion crawling up his cowboy boot. Brushing it aside, he said, "This here scorpion is one of the strongest animals in Big Bend. Why, the other night in the bunkhouse down in the Chisos Basin one of these little fellows got in bed with my partner who weighs 180 pounds. He maneuvered around until he got at my partner's rear end. Then, without further ado, he lifted that 180-pound man clean off the bed."

Jim Bowmer, lawyer of Temple, Texas, spoke up:

"One of them critters almost ruined a wedding."

"How come?"

"The preacher discovered he had one in his breeches as he started to perform a wedding ceremony."

"What happened?"

"It was the fastest wedding in Texas history. Even so, the preacher got bit seven times."

That night we camped on Blue Creek on the western slopes of the Chisos Range. The bunch grass was thick, though we were close to the zone where greasewood takes over. We were far below the tree line, cactus and an occasional scrub juniper making up the only shrubs. Blue Creek once had a spring which Homer Wilson, a cattleman, tapped, bringing water some eight miles down to his ranch home. But that spring sanded in and vandals carried away his pipes. Other springs in the Blue Creek Canyon had also sanded up, leaving no water for man or for wild life. So we packed our water—for drinking and for cooking.

We stayed at the old Wilson rock house, a structure that the National Park Service will convert into a museum. The midday sun is hot, even in early May, and the rocks of Blue Creek and the galvanized roof of the ranch house are refectory ovens. But with the lowering sun a wind came up.

The windows of the rock house were now only gaping holes where the wind whined. The rock walls of the house once had been covered with stucco which now was badly worn by wind and weather. There is an open porch or gallery without a railing, facing east. The winds that had come from time out of mind from the northwest had carried sand on their wings; and the posts supporting the roof of the porch looked as if they had been scoured. I lay on the edge of the porch watching the scrub. A jack rabbit stomped not far from the house. A kangaroo rat scooted under the porch. The wind picked up and I could see the sand moving under its relentless pressure, rolling by me an inch or so a minute. An owl flew noiselessly by. High over some cliffs a vulture circled. There was no other sign of life.

Buck Newsom, the genial Texan who brought us to Blue Creek, sat on his heels telling tall tales of the Big Bend country.

He told us about a cowboy who was "addicted to getting as drunk as a biled owl."

It seems that this cowboy maintained a lonely vigil at the Wilson ranch, seeing no one for weeks on end. Today a Park Service's paved road lies to the north of an adjoining ridge, not more than a half-mile distant. But in those days Blue Creek was in desolate isolation. The cowboy, rummaging around the store-room of the ranch house, found a bottle of whiskey. He repaired at once to the front porch and slowly sipped the liquor. As he drank, the dreary scenery brightened, his cares sloughed off, his despondency disappeared, and a new, strange buoyancy possessed him. Finishing the bottle, he rose, stretched his arms to the sky, and shouted,

"I wish I was *some* place."

Most Texans love their land with a real passion. Their affection extends to the relic forests and the colima warblers and the cactus and scorpions, too. The creation of the park has given new security to botanical life that in the 1930s seemed almost extinct. In spite of drought the land is now coming back and regaining an ecological balance. The young firs, pines, and cypress at Boot Spring Camp are partial proof of it. The bunch grass that is returning on the dry slopes of Blue Creek is further evidence. The idea was summed up by Buck Newsom at our camp on Blue Creek: "This land promises less and gives you more than any other land. Turn these horses loose and they'll get fat as hogs on this bunch grass."

The Big Bend National Park shows the regenerative force of nature even under desertic conditions once the despoilers are kept from the land. Staggering problems, however, remain, as we shall see. This is fragile land and can easily be destroyed even by those who walk reverently. And the philosophy of Adam Smith is so dominant in Texas that opposition to the establishment of other like national parks is fierce and unrelenting. The land in the Big Bend National Park was so worn out by owners, who pounded and despoiled it, that "bailing them out" through government acquisition became attractive by entrepreneurial standards. So far, that has been the sure formula for creating recreational enclaves.

CHAPTER III

THE DRY EARTH

Some seventy miles north of Big Bend National Park, the West Texas towns of Alpine, Marathon, and Marfa form a triangle enclosing an area famous for its good grass and its salubrious climate. They lie in the 5,000-foot zone above sea level and thus escape the searing heat of the Chihuahua Desert. The nights are cool and the days mostly clear. The climate is still salubrious, but much of the land is being pounded by overgrazing and turned from good grass to sand and scrub.

Records of rainfall have been kept at Alpine for only twenty-four years, and the readings at Alpine may be meaningless 20 miles away at Marfa or Marathon or in the National Park to the south. For showers in this country are erratic phenomena that leave one side of a valley drought-ridden and the other refreshed by rain. No one knows for sure what the average rainfall in an area is. But, in the vicinity of Alpine, Marathon, and Marfa it is estimated to be somewhere in the neighborhood of 15 inches a year.

While 15 inches is enough for good grass if the soil is undisturbed, the dryness attracts cacti, of which Texas probably has more species than Arizona. A little old lady from Ohio walked the open lands out of Alpine searching out cactus specimens.

And when she had made her selection and carefully boxed them for carriage back home, she dropped by the office of Jim Glasscock, editor of Alpine's weekly newspaper, *The Alpine Avalanche,* and took out a year's subscription. The editor thanked her for her interest in Alpine's affairs.

"Oh, it's not that," she replied. "I only want to know when it rains in Alpine so I can water my cactus in Ohio."

If the rainfall here is difficult to estimate, it is even more difficult to predict. Of its unpredictability the late J. Frank Dobie said: "Nobody but a fool or a newcomer will prophesy weather in Texas," only to add the traveler's retort that "fools and newcomers were the only kind of people he had seen since coming to Texas."

John C. Duval wrote in his short story, "Old Prob's Visit to Texas," about a peon warning government meteorologists of a severe storm not predicted by any of their instruments. The storm came in a flash, wiping out their camp; and after they had found refuge in the peon's hunt, they learned how he had predicted it.

"Sirs," he explained, not without pride, "my burro told me everything. When a storm is coming, he keeps his tail toward it. If it is going to hail, he puts his head far down. If the storm is not going to be very bad, he has his tail against a pine tree; but if it is going to be fierce, he keeps his tail against my house. His tail has been against my house for many hours."

Rainstorms in the Big Bend country are something to behold. The air is fragrant when the rain starts to fall. The odor of dust being watered down fills the countryside. It is a tantalizing odor filled with expectancy that marks an end of a drought and promises the commencement of new life. Rain on the desert supplants despair with hope and promises a better life for tomorrow.

There is no rain that is regional. Rains come in local showers that may cover a few acres or a few sections. It is customary to see four or five on different points of the compass. They sometimes come gently, sometimes with a vengeance. The downpour can be heavy, pouring inches of icy water on dry land in less than an hour. On these occasions one can stand on the edge of the storm in dry sunshine and put out one's hand into a torrent. "It's as if a wall of bluish-green water pours out of the sky an arm's length away," Peter Koch of Alpine says.

There is a saying in West Texas that "crop estimates will be exceeded if it rains till the moisture meets." And when a big storm is brewing they say, "Looks like A rain is needed." When it starts pouring the West Texans say, "A gully washer is needed with rain coming down in sheets."

These rains run from May to September. They bring spectacular lightning that fills the sky with flashes and strikes with vengeance in forked tongues. Basket grass, as I have said, is particularly volatile; it is not a conspicuous target for lightning, but a goodly number of lightning fires are started in it; and it burns with a vengeance.

A more likely target is a stalk of yucca or sotol that may grow eight feet high or more. Once, on Gage Holland's Hell's Half Acre Ranch, I saw lightning hit a sotol stalk with the speed of a rattlesnake. Indians used the sotol to make signal fires. This particular sotol burst into flames like a match and burned for a half-hour with sparkling brilliance. Then it died out in the rain. By and large these desert fires are not devastating.

Flash floods present a more serious threat. The over-all rainfall is so low and the climate so arid that drainage has developed no rivers. Arroyos that are dry most of the time are without number.

A light half-hour rain can start a small stream running in a dry arroyo; a hard 15-minute rain can start a torrent. Continuous rains—even off-and-on rains—can fill a dry arroyo with a roaring wall of water. Thus, today, wherever a highway crosses a gully, the state has erected a gauge showing up to five feet the depth of the flood and warning motorists of the danger of being trapped midstream.

When water goes on that kind of desert rampage, great damage can be done. When the turf is firm and the grass cover healthy, these downpours are mostly absorbed. But where overgrazing has taken place, the bare mineral soil is exposed. Then a downpour washes the precious minerals into the arroyo and grassland becomes desert. That's what happened to Tornillo Flats where people once mowed hay.

In order to deal with this problem, ranchers these days create impoundments by erecting earthen dams across arroyos. Some of these ponds last the winter through and have water until the rains start again. It is today a common practice to build low dams that will divert water into the shoulders of the arroyo where the ground is disked and Johnson grass is planted. After several years the Johnson grass is also disked to encourage the spread of its root systems. In this way ranchers use flood waters to raise supplementary food for their Herefords.

The most common way of increasing water supply is by the windmill, which first came into use on a large scale in 1873 on the plains. The first one reached the Big Bend from Chicago in 1885; and their number has vastly multiplied. Ranchers go down on the average from 100 to 200 feet for their windmill water and pump it out into huge metallic tanks. These feed lower-set watering tanks whose level is controlled by floats that close a valve at a high level and open it at a low one.

"Water witching," to determine sites for windmills, is common in the Big Bend. Some practitioners prefer mesquite. Others bring willow or the fork of a fruit tree. Some prefer malleable copper strips.

"And some will settle for a metal coathanger," Gage Holland of Hell's Half Acre told me.

The water-witching average of success is very high in the Big Bend and masters of the art are in great demand. For water on a Big Bend ranch is like gold in the bank. It not only supplies livestock, it also services wild life; and these days, as I have said, wild life has important commercial aspects to the ranchers. The business of renting land to hunters is a new one that in the end will probably prove more profitable than cattle. However that may be, this significant source of cash income is made possible by windmills that supply water to attract the deer and keep them on the place.

Water in this desert country is fickle. The available supply is not in an aquifer representing a pool collected over the eons. The supply is probably made up from local drainage, which means that the establishment of the park has created problems. A headquarters requires several dozens of homes for personnel. A park attracts concessionaires who will cater to the needs of the public. This means water for tens of thousands of people.

So far the problem has not been acute. But the Park Service has tapped four wells that supply Chisos Basin—Oak Springs averaging six to eight gallons a minute, Cattail Falls averaging eight to 10, and two wells from CCC days that average 14 gallons a minute. To supply park headquarters there are three wells, from 78 to 217 feet deep, that produce from four to 20 gallons a minute. Whether there is any connection with these wells is not known, but in recent years historic springs have dried up and game has had to go many more miles for its supply. The Park Service is the first to realize the critical nature of the problem and has alternative plans to use the Rio Grande that marks the southern border of the Big Bend National Park for all water for official and tourist use.

Most of the park at one time was a sotol-grass community below, say, 4,800 feet. Overgrazing eliminated much of the grass and desert scrub took over. But there are islands today in the

3,000–4,000-foot zone where tobosa grass, the three-awn grasses, and the grama grasses flourish with the sotol.

The lower zones are desert scrub. This is where the creosote bush, lechuguilla, Spanish dagger, and tarbush flourish. Ocotillo, showing red flags in May, is also found here. Overgrazing has had its most damaging effects in these two lower areas. Acre after acre shows bare mineral soil with no grasses left—nothing but creosote or Spanish dagger, or tarbush.

Seventy-five per cent of the days are cloudless and only rarely do entirely cloudy days occur. The soil seldom freezes below a depth of one inch. In February, temperatures within the root zone range from 52 degrees to 65 degrees—sufficiently high to promote growth. Surface temperatures of 100 degrees and more occur late in April or May, ranging as high as 116 degrees in

June. In June, soil temperatures a foot below the surface range from 85 degrees to 92 degrees. In these hot periods the evaporation rate is high, about twice what it is on the short-grass plains of Colorado. At that rate only a relatively scant plant population of xeric species can endure. When the pounding of hoofs is added, it is a miracle if all grass does not disappear; and that tragedy is the trend in West Texas. The grama grasses go early, being replaced by the burro grass that is quite unpalatable but produces an abundance of seeds and flower stalks in dry weather. Its very shallow, wide-spreading roots enable it to thrive when only the first inch of soil is moistened. The weedy watchweed also comes in on overgrazing, and it is not grazed. Hence, it thrives on the excess water when grass is closely cropped. The mesquite also comes in as a result of overgrazing—and cactus,

too. At the higher elevations a piñon-juniper woodland invasion is a telltale sign of too much pressure on grass.

That has happened to most of the Big Bend country in and out of the park. And today it continues to deplete much of the land outside the park.

Some of this man-made desert was created last century before there was fencing. The lack of fencing was part of the early problem of overgrazing. West Texas did not have the timber for the eastern type of rail fence. Fencing became a burning issue— between cattlemen and farmers, between one cattleman who claimed a range and a rival whose cattle invaded it. In Texas the planting of hedges was proposed—hedges made from a rose that "required little trimming, did not spread, would turn cattle, was ornamental and fragrant, and would furnish feed for cows

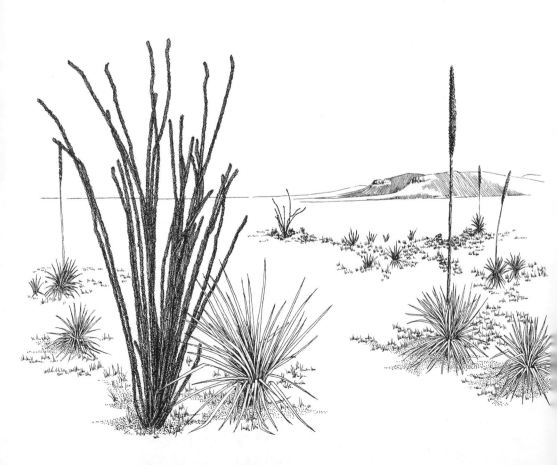

and strip the fur from a rabbit" (Webb, *The Great Plains,* p. 294).

Then, in 1878, came barbed wire and the plains were revolutionized. Barbed wire came from Illinois but the plains became its principal market. It caused a disappearance of the open, free range and converted the range country into big-pasture country. It made possible, therefore, the introduction of blooded stock that needed care and surveillance. That sounded the death knell of the Longhorn. It also started the trend toward conservation, or at least made it possible. With fences there was now a method of rotating cattle so that one pasture could rest while others were being grazed.

But these fences, although of conservational value, were a matter of concern to botanists, as Bedichek relates in *Adventures with a Texas Naturalist,* for they changed radically the flora native to the region. One who combs a cow pasture for botanical specimens finds fewer in the pasture than on the other side of the fence. Cattle cause a great reduction in species; goats are much more severe; but sheep practically obliterate flowers, leaving only shrubs and grass. Native flowers need to bloom in order to reproduce and do not survive rigorous grazing. The naturalist in Texas, therefore, finds his greatest variety of flowers in two man-made enclaves: railroad rights of way and fence-protected rights of way for highways.

The threat to the plant life of the range might have been minimized by a careful rotation of stock. But the conservational potentialities of the barbed-wire fence were never realized. Even after the arrival of the barbed-wire pastures the land was abused; there was overgrazing—overgrazing by reason of overstocking the range. World War I, with its high cattle prices, led to overstocked ranges in West Texas. So did World War II. After World War II the rains made hundreds of sections green. But cattle were followed by sheep and goats, and sheep and goats by desert.

The early 1960s brought a prolonged drought in West Texas and low cattle prices. The poor pasture conditions that resulted forced ranchers to purchase more feed than usual, at higher than usual prices. Moreover, the drought resulted in lowering the marketing weights of the cattle and calves. These forces combined to drive the net income for cattle ranches downward. In this area it averaged $1,310 in 1964, the lowest level since 1956. Net income for sheep ranchers in the area averaged $3,258 in 1964. This was a drastic drop even though the prices of lambs and wool were higher in 1964 than they had been for several years. Ranch costs increased; feed costs mounted; and ranchers who reduced their breeding flocks because of the drought had fewer lambs to sell in 1964.

Hundreds of sections of land in West Texas are now denuded permanently—in the sense that several generations will never see their restoration. By human accounting, a land converted to desert in an area of 15 inches of rainfall is a permanent desert. The Big Bend country is a monument to free enterprise that was unrestrained and private initiative that knew no standard except greed. The Big Bend country shows how predatory man can make an area desolate.

"What kind of man would pound this barren land into dust?" I asked.

"One stingy enough to skin a flea for its hide and tallow, even while toting around a wad you could choke a cow with," Peter Koch replied.

The truth is that, while this is good country for light grazing, it is so fragile it cannot withstand the heavy use which it now receives. The ranchers are mostly marginal, working largely to make the interest on their bank loans. The land continues to depreciate. The time may come when the present owners (and their bankers) will want to be "bailed out." It is probably only then that the land can be put to its highest use—recreation.

CHAPTER IV

CANYONS OF THE

RIO GRANDE

The Rio Grande became the fixed boundary between us and Mexico in 1848 by the Treaty of Guadalupe Hidalgo, from the Gulf to the southern border of New Mexico.

This great river is second only to the Mississippi–Missouri system in the United States. It rises nearly three miles above sea level in Colorado and winds itself eastward and then south to bisect New Mexico. It is a clear river until it nears Albuquerque. There it begins to pick up silt and for the rest of its journey to the Gulf of Mexico it is heavy most of the time with the soil of our Southwest.

From prehistoric days, when only the Indians knew the river, the water was diverted for irrigation wherever a shoulder of land could be reached by ditches. Modern dams, irrigation, and extensive use of water have reduced the river to a dry arroyo west of Presidio, Texas. It indeed dies in a desert only to be resurrected by the Rio Conchos, which comes roaring out of the mountains of Mexico to refill the river.

Those who run the Rio Grande in Texas ride along on Mexican water.

Some of its most interesting waters are between Stillwell Crossing on east to Langtry, Texas. Starting at that Crossing the river immediately enters Heath Canyon and then quickly pours into open country, fairly uninteresting until La Linda and a fluorspar plant are reached. From this point on the river funnels into a narrow canyon about 2,000 feet deep that Robert T. Hill of the Geological Survey in 1899 called Temple Canyon. The water is fast and ideal for canoes and kayaks. Beyond Temple Canyon is Maravillas Creek where the mountains have pulled back a few miles on either side of the river, giving startling views of desert and peaks, including Castle Butte in Mexico. This is a stretch of fewer rapids and many long pools of quiet water. Big Canyon comes quickly, with what Bob Burleson calls swift water and "boulder gardens." There follows another canyon perhaps 40 miles long (Reagan) with the fastest water yet and blind turns and twists that add to the excitement. There are places where canoes have to be "lined" through, i.e., lowered by a line, and other stretches where the only passage is by portage. There are hot springs galore in this area. Burro Bluff shows towering cliffs on the Texas side with some rapids safe only for "lining" a canoe and others safe only for portage. Waterfall Rapids, where the river drops about eight feet at once, is also a place of portage. In 40 miles the walls get lower and lower but they are still beautiful, being fashioned of white limestone. The country opens up only to close again, as a narrow canyon forms that runs 15 miles to the Davenport Ranch, a good take-out point.

Frank X. Tolbert described the adventures in this section of the Rio Grande of a party headed by Bob Burleson, president of the Texas Explorers Club:

"Bill Kugle, Bob Burleson, and several other lawyer types, including Neil Caldwell, Charlie Arnold, and Davis Bragg, recently went on what turned out to be a four-day canoe trip in the Rio Grande, from Stillwell's Crossing near the Big Bend National Park to just upstream from Langtry, Judge Roy Bean's old seat of justice in Val Verde County.

"President Burleson paddled serenely downstream, Kugle, Arnold, and Neil Caldwell, who is a state legislator from Alvin, had all sorts of weird adventures. Kugle, who was in a kayak, ended the trip completely in the nude, which he said caused the first human type he'd seen (other than his legal companions) in four days, a Mexican urchin near Langtry, to call his mamma: 'Mother, a naked gringo comes in a small boat.'

"The troubles of Kugle, Arnold, and Caldwell are too numerous to chronicle in this space. The second day out, Arnold and Caldwell flipped their canoe and ruined the expedition's only movie

camera. Worst of all, in midwinter, Charlie's sleeping bag was soaked.

"Astoundingly he found another! The sides of the canyons were honeycombed with thousands of little caves. Arnold went into one of them to build a fire, and perhaps sleep there while his clothes dried during the night. (It would be days before the sleeping bag lost its sogginess.) And there in the first cave he entered was a dry bedroll and mackinaw wrapped in a rope! Perhaps some unfortunate explorer had left the stuff there years ago, yet it was still serviceable.

"Before they ended the saga, Arnold and Caldwell flipped their canoe again in one of the many violent rapids and lost most of their food and got all wet again. Bill Kugle was nearly drowned when his kayak got away from him and he had to swim after it in a mighty current. And with no dry clothes, that's how he happened to finish the voyage in the nude.

"Six days after leaving Stillwell's Crossing, Kugle was in Del Rio in his pickup truck, wearing only some shorts and socks. The rest of his clothes he'd either lost in the raging rapids or they were too wet to put on. He drove up to a drive-in and offered the waitress a wet $10 bill after ordering a beer.

"Don't you have change?' asked the girl.

"'Lady, I don't even have any pants,' replied Bill."

Everyone has his own favorite section of the river and mine are three canyons farther upstream that fall on the border of the Big Bend National Park—Boquillas on the eastern side, Mariscal at the southern tip, and Santa Elena at the western corner.

At these points the river cut its path through mountain ranges rather than around them, carving out three deep canyons.

Mariscal Canyon makes the Big Bend for which the region is named. It turns the Rio Grande from a southeast course to one running northeast. The cut is nearly 2,000 feet deep and about seven miles long; and it is often no more than 100 feet wide. The canyon gets its name from the mountain it bisects. Mariscal Mountain is mostly limestone. From top to bottom the sculpturing was done by water or water-borne abrasives, the river literally cutting its present path out of solid rock.

I stood on its banks shivering in the gray dawn of a Texas winter day. A cold wind came out of the north and it blew so hard that the sand at my feet formed into ripples. Sand stung my cheeks; the greasewood bowed before the gale.

I had seen the Rio Grande from planes high over Colorado and New Mexico and had crossed it by car at Presidio, Texas, going into Mexico. But I had never been on it. I had seen it mostly when it was heavy with silt and this January day was no exception, for it had a brownish-slate color.

The place was Panterra, which has no sign, no building to mark it—a spot where once there was a farm but which now stands in desolate isolation about 30 feet above the river. We came with Bob Burleson and Jim Bowmer of Temple, Texas, Davis Bragg and Bill Dean of Killeen, Texas, and Bill Thompson of Houston. Panterra was our starting point for running Mariscal Canyon. Our rubber rafts and our duffel were scattered along the bluff. Fisherman were camped at Panterra, and the high wind blew the sparks from their mesquite fire into the brush. These men had driven hundreds of miles to try their luck at catfish. Channel cat are in the Rio Grande and they run up to 20 pounds. These fishermen, however, talked about the Rio Grande catfish that is gray, rather than yellow, and runs up to 120 pounds. "Makes as fine a steak as pompano," one bearded fisherman told me. "Almost as good as pompano," his companion added.

These fishermen had a great respect for the river, and when they found that a few wives were along, they tried to dissuade us from running the river. "Are you sure you know what you folks are getting into?" "Are these women good swimmers?" "Don't you know there's an eight-foot waterfall you have to go over?" The bearded one rubbed his chin and said, "Not for love nor money would I do it." With that he brewed up a pot of coffee especially for us, telling us it would probably be our last cup.

The day before we had scouted both our entrance route and our exit route to the river. This is the Chihuahua Desert that rolls on and on in an undulating plain. Black-topped Highways 118 and 385 come down from Alpine and Marathon respectively to Big Bend National Park. Route 170, also hard-topped, reaches the park from Presidio. The park—encircled on the south by the Rio Grande—has hard-surfaced roads on its perimeter and a few into its interior. But almost every access road to the river is dirt.

The Davis Mountains are far to the northwest, the Chisos to the north, both having a purplish cast. Pieces of broken mountain ridges stand in barren isolation. This is gullied country covered with greasewood, sotol, yucca, and cactus and streaked with long fingers of low mesquite trees that in moonlight are reminiscent of peach orchards. But in daylight hours this is sun-drenched country where the temperatures march to 120°F. in the summer and 70°F. in the winter. Jack rabbits are common. Lizards and race runners (but not many snakes) can be found in the hot months. An eagle may be occasionally seen soaring. Hawks and vultures are present year round. There are coyotes who still roam the Chihuahua Desert in spite of man's incessant poisoning programs and they are heard at night.

This cold January morning at Panterra, I saw mule deer crossing the river to Mexico. But on all my travels there I have seen little life. While a height of land shows purple mountains in the distance, the roads show mostly mile after mile of gray monotony and little movement of game.

These dirt roads have high centers and deep ruts but very few signs. That is why we try to get familiar with them by day, for in the dark they are swallowed up by the greasewood and sand.

When we run this section of the Rio Grande in Texas we are on waters that quite a few people float. The Park Service estimates that some 1,500 people run one or more of the three canyons each year. But historically this was a river to ford, not to float.

It was first visited at its mouth in the Gulf in the fall of 1519 by four Spanish ships out of Jamaica under Captain Alonso Alvarez de Pineda and was then called the River of the Palms because of the trees growing in its delta. (The native palm, *Sabal texana*, is endemic to a small area in southernmost Texas— Cameron County—and adjacent Tamaulipas State, Mexico, and is now near the point of extermination.) In later years, other fleets explored its mouth, some going upstream 20 miles or more in search of a passage to the Orient. A side-wheeler called the *Ariel*, owned by Stephen Austin, plied the lower reaches beginning in 1829, going as far upriver as Revella but mostly carrying freight between Matamoras and Camargo. In those days—long before modern irrigation projects—the river was always filled with water, the problem being to find a ford where a pack train could cross it. But even when the river was full, its rapids made it non-navigable for sizable vessels and hazardous for smaller ones.

These Texas canyons were run by Robert T. Hill of the Geological Survey, in 1899, and prior to him by one James Mac-Mahon, who trapped for beaver. All earlier attempts failed, the International Boundary Survey calling them impassable. Hill used flat-bottomed boats. I prefer canoes or rubber rafts except for Santa Elena, where only a raft should be used.

Panterra, where we met the fishermen, is the start of a journey into Mariscal Canyon and is about three miles above its mouth, affording one a chance to get accustomed to his craft before the first big roar is heard short of the canyon—a six-foot drop through a stretch of rapids that is negotiated in a few seconds. Ahead are several folds in the hills and at least three cracks in Mariscal Mountain. But no one can identify the gorge until he is practically in it. A very loud roar is a miscue. It marks another rapids whose roar is amplified by a box canyon that joins the river from the Texas side. Then comes the canyon proper—the river flows right, then bends left, and there is the canyon with a sand bar on the left, where we made a landfall for pictures.

The walls shoot up to a dizzy height, the river fills the narrow passage from wall to wall, and then disappears in a sharp turn to the left behind the vertical crack. There was the feeling of finality when I entered the canyon because I knew we could not leave it short of the other end.

"Let's go back," someone said from the head of a raft. "Too late," I shouted. I felt the sucking river pulling my raft into the gorge with the power of an irresistible magnet and I knew, as one in a space ship must feel when he leaves the launching pad, that an irreversible commitment had been made.

Some have lost their craft and worked their way out. In Boquillas that would not be too difficult. In Mariscal and Santa Elena it's well-nigh impossible.

William H. Emory, who made the first boundary survey in the 1850s, called these canyons "gorges of frightful sublimity." Parts are frightful; some are sublime.

About one-third mile inside Mariscal Canyon is an ancient rock barrier where a jumble of huge boulders fills the stream bed, leaving only cracks for water and boats. Unless the water is very high, a landfall can be made on the left or Texas side above the rockslide where a gravel bar has been deposited. From this vantage point a low-level appraisal of the slide area can be made and a passage selected. The one to the left is the widest and best for canoes but it often contains snags that can be dangerous to rubber rafts. Passage to the right is in the shape of a narrow, roaring

"S" where the river pours into and around huge rocks. That was the course to take, I decided.

We were all in rafts and some lady, holding her paddle high, merely screamed. Screaming is not the best technique for making a perfect letter "S" in white water. But somehow or other we all made it and escaped the fate of ending on edge against one of the rocks in the turbulent water.

A quarter-mile farther down is the area Bob Burleson properly calls the "tight squeeze." There is a "gentleman's turn" in the river that ends at a solid wall of stone. It seems for a second that the river has gone underground. Then a four-foot passageway appears on the Texas side and a seven-foot passageway on the right. Each is a blind entry, but the one on the Mexican side is the only possible way.

We took it. I felt the powerful sucking of the river. I heard a woman's scream. I paddled like mad on the right; the rubber raft lightly scraped the huge rock and in less time than it takes to write this, we were in the open.

Some of the cliffs look like yellowish marble which reflected sunlight turns reddish and direct sunlight, golden. Erosion of water and wind has produced castellated and turreted forms. Some walls show acres of yellow where gargantuan chips have broken off. The black top of carbon stain of decomposed plants of Mariscal is underlain by pinkish streaks. Lichens have painted some sections in somber grays and greens; others, in bright red and bright yellow. There are a few moist spots high on these walls where water may spout in the wet season. But the walls are mostly dry, showing ledges and setbacks where some ferns and pineapple plants grow. The narrow sections close in on man, emphasizing that escape is by the river. It would indeed require pitons, ropes, and great expertise to climb the walls of Mariscal.

Mariscal Canyon is almost two canyons in one, for it breaks in the middle. It is there that an ancient Indian and smuggler's trail crosses. On the Mexican side are adobe huts thatched with cane—now unoccupied but once the headquarters for smuggling operations. Ancient Indian petroglyphs are pecked into two large boulders at the mouth of a creek on the Mexican side.

The second half of the canyon has fast water but no rapids of consequence.

Once we stopped on a gravel bar and I lay against the raft looking downstream. The brownish-slate color of the river made the blue of the sky seem even more brilliant than those bright skies that are regularly produced by the Southwest. Between the river and the sky were a medley of colors—white, red, gray, brown, and black. The deepening shadows changed their tints to soft pastels and then, as dusk thickened, the brightness of the walls faded and the colors were erased, and I was in a deep canyon of monotones.

The last fourth of the canyon has a long stretch of open water with high walls around it where the acoustics are perfect. One can overhear a quiet conversation at a distance of 200 yards. Water dripping from paddles is audible for 50 yards. Any dripping water sounds, indeed, like little bells. Bill Dean decided to exploit these acoustics with his paddle so as to produce a rifle shot. He came down so hard that he produced a startling effect; but he also broke his paddle into three pieces and had only the stick of a paddle to make the remaining few miles to our take-out point at Solis where in ancient days Indians used river water to raise melons and corn.

For the run of the Boquillas Canyon—farthest east of the three and easiest to run—we put in below the Mexican village of the same name and in a mile or less were at the mouth of the canyon proper. There are some sheer walls that rise 800 feet or so and they dominate the first few miles. Then come some four miles of open canyon with small valleys and high buttes that sit back a half-mile from the river. Pointing to a huge rock delicately balanced on a pinnacle of rock several hundred feet above the water, I said to Bob Burleson, "The vibration of one rifle shot would cause it to come tumbling down." Water and water-borne abrasives have carved gargantuan caves at the river's edge. Higher up are other caverns, deep, dark, and largely unexplored. We beached our rafts below one cave large enough to hold a motorcar and scrambled up a talus slope to it. To our surprise it contained bats and from it we collected a pound or more of bat guano. (There are at least 17 species of bats in the park.) Donovan Correll—noted Texas botanist who was in the party—exclaimed, "What an excellent fertilizer for house plants!" The length of Boquillas proper is about 12 miles and it can be done in a day. But two days or even three are the way to enjoy it.

I love the flat sandbanks of the Boquillas that lie above the winter water level. These benches are covered with Bermuda grass; and the beaver that inhabit the canyon have usually left a supply of cut branches for firewood. I like to lie on my back watching clouds race over the crack in the sky formed by the sheer canyon walls. There are swifts under the cliffs; and the mud nests of the rough-winged swallow are thick under the overhangs. Gray-breasted gnatcatchers and black phoebes streak across the water. Green-winged teal and black ducks move downstream ahead of one. American ravens are nesting, and several pair are far overhead, soaring silently toward the cliffs. And somewhere high on the walls is the canyon wren—reddish-brown with a conspicuous white throat—whose song is the liveliest one in Texas. The song—*te-you, te-you, te-you, tew, tew, tew, tew, tew*—comes tripping down the scale.

There is the sound of the river, too—the quiet, gurgling sound nearby and ahead the distant roar of cascades. This is the place for reveries.

The banks of Boquillas are thick with stands of carrizo or common reed (*Phragmites*) and giant reed.

"Bulrushes," someone exclaimed. "Like the ones along the Nile where they found Moses."

They do indeed contain life. Birds frequent the cane; rabbits hide there; and deer bed down. Don Correll explained to me that the giant reed, the culm of which is used in Europe for making the reeds of clarinets, was imported by the Spanish. The common reed is native; and the two are usually together in mixed stands. The reed is good forage for cattle, quite a few being run in the Boquillas Canyon. So the habit of the ranchers is to burn it in the winter with the idea of getting fresh, tender shoots by spring. That is why Boquillas is sometimes filled with smoke. I first saw the honey tree (*Huisache*) in the Boquillas. Salt cedars (*Tamarix*) and black willow, common around the globe, thrive there. I also found a wild persimmon with fruit the size of a penny that is black and very sweet. Small mesquite is scattered. But apart from the two reeds, the most conspicuous is the dark-leaved tobacco tree (*Nicotiana*) which by February is showing yellow flowers. The wood we used the most for fires was from the tobacco tree; and it burns with a high flame, while the mesquite, like all locust trees, burns with steady, intense heat.

It was a clear, cool day when we ran the Boquillas. When the sun came up, the wind dropped and by noon I was comfortable paddling in shirt sleeves. We beached the canoe at every point where there was evidence that the canyon had been peopled. Boquillas—unlike the other two—shows much evidence that it has been. Some benches are indeed small valleys where coveys of the blue quail abound. On my visit these benches were gaily painted with the yellow blossoms of the evening primrose. The mustards added pinkish colors. The resurrection plant, whose spires always point north, abounds. The pineapple plant (*Hechtia*) grows high on the canyon walls. Texas, which is said to have even more species of cacti than Arizona, puts many on display in Boquillas Canyon. Conspicuous is the strawberry cactus whose fruit is the size of a golf ball and very sweet.

In the late afternoon, when the canyon was in complete shadow, I rounded a bend to see through a notch in a canyon wall the distant Sierra del Carmen Range in Mexico. The lowering sun was drenching it in a light cerise color.

Its sheer cliffs were brilliant draperies in the lowering sun. But they disappeared as quickly as they had appeared, a bend in the canyon erasing them from view.

At that point smoke filled the canyon—smoke from four fires on the Mexico side, attended by a dozen or more men. We beached our boat and went ashore to see firsthand some rather primitive wax-manufacturing plants guarded by armed Mexicans.

I talked to one Mexican with dancing eyes and a bushy mustache. His straw sombrero was on the back of his head; he wore crude sandals; and his shirt and trousers had not been laundered for weeks. He spoke a bit of English and explained with the help of Don Correll, the botanist, what was going on.

Candelilla is a spurge, known as the wax plant. Smooth pencil-sized stems grow in a cluster from a common stock and stand a foot or so high. It grows exclusively in the Chihuahua Desert in a rather narrow belt on each side of the river. The stems have a thin veneer of wax that is thickest in the extremes of weather. That wax is prized for chewing gum, candles, phonograph records, shoe polish, and floor wax.

The Mexican explained how they pull up the plant by the roots and stack it on burros in big bundles and carry them to the crude wax plants that consist of a cauldron over a pit where a hot fire of the sotol bush burns. The cauldron contains water and sulphuric acid and the wax is reduced when that liquid boils.

I saw several men using dippers to take liquid off the surface of the cauldrons, pouring it in a depression in the ground where the earth had been dampened. There it quickly hardened into a brittle mass that could be broken into smaller bits for loading into gunny sacks, to be transported to another plant for more complete refining.

My mustached friend accommodated me by breaking a piece off with a rock and presenting me with it.

I later learned from the Park Service that it is unlawful to cut candelilla in the park and that there are constant patrols to prevent it. Some poaching takes place. But there are some stretches of land outside the park, including barren-looking peaks, where the plant flourishes.

I also later learned from Apache Adams, who then lived at Stillwell Crossing not far below Boquillas Canyon, that he hired crews to collect the plant on private lands. They reduce it in crude wax plants such as those we saw in Mexico. The problem of gathering and reducing the candelilla on the American side presents no legal difficulty. If a Mexican collects it in this country and carries it to Mexico, there is no problem of export or import. But there is a problem once the wax is reduced in Mexico. The Bank of Mexico claims a monopoly over it. If wax is exported to this country, a duty must be paid. But this duty is high and methods of evasion are notorious. Apache Adams processed 10,000 pounds a month, and of that no more than 5 per cent was Mexican. How much is processed in northern Mexico I do not know. But it is said that wax income keeps that poverty-ridden area from starvation. It is hard work, as sometimes one must pull up 1,000 pounds of plants for 30 pounds of wax.

The Mexicans who attended the cauldrons in Boquillas Canyon were a happy lot. Their food was the roasted starchy heart of the sotol bush. They returned to Boquillas village every Sunday. The other six days they climbed to the peaks for the wax plant and moved their cauldrons to convenient locations. The open bowl-like Boquillas Canyon is ideal for this operation. Mariscal—

the next canyon upstream—has only one crossing. There on another day we had seen piles of candelilla 20 feet high, awaiting hot cauldrons.

We camped overnight not far below the wax cauldrons. It was what Emory would have called a "delicious twilight." The sun slowly crept up canyon walls until the sundial showed six o'-clock. The clouds were still in the spotlight; but when they passed, the sky turned gray and a short twilight possessed us. Fierce winds often whip the canyon, especially at night. Bob Burleson, Jim Bowmer, and Davis Bragg have had bitter experiences with high night winds. Once in Boquillas Canyon, while the party slept on the Mexican side, a powerful wind picked up a four-man rubber raft and whipped it across the river to Texas. If a tent or lean-to is pitched lengthwise with the canyon, a strong night wind can demolish it. That is why our shelters are always pitched cross-canyon.

This night we made lean-tos, Bob Burleson supplying canoe paddles for uprights. We fastened our tarps at the lower end to stakes and at the entrance draped them over guy ropes running from the canoe paddle. We were soon snug against wind and rain.

We built a fire of the tobacco-tree wood, conveniently left by beavers, and dragged in mesquite for coals for cooking steaks. The fires were soon burning brightly and the smell of freshly brewed coffee filled the canyon. The bullfrogs first started their chorus; then came the rock frogs. Occasionally I heard the booming slap of a beaver's tail. Soon a three-quarter moon rose over the canyon, casting an eerie light. We had steaming coffee and steaks cooked by Peter Koch in the coals of mesquite wood. Hermes Nye—Texas lawyer and folksinger—produced his guitar and a goodly number of voices joined him to produce haunting melodies in this remote canyon. But we were asleep rather early. This turned out to be the warmest night in the canyon, for no wind at all came up and we would have been comfortable had we merely put our bedrolls down in the open.

The sun did not rise above the high canyon walls until nearly eleven o'clock the next day. Brahman cattle crossed and recrossed the river ahead of us, sometimes swimming. Many burros appeared on the Mexican side. The walls were sheer, the water mostly calm, the air chill in the enveloping shade of the canyon.

We always wear life jackets on the river because the rapids are swift, the pools deep, and the winter water cold. They are awkward and warmish on clear, lazy days, but accidents do happen even to the cautious. A hidden snag can instantly deflate a raft; a canoe can capsize or be swamped in white water. The Boquillas offers few risks of the latter kind. When there are only a few head feet of water, only one watercourse offers problems. It is in the lower third of the canyon at Maruffo Vega and is known historically as The Ruffian. The drop is about six feet; and the danger lies in a huge rock about 75 feet from the lip of the falls around which the river flows to the left. One has to paddle strenuously on the right to keep his canoe from foundering on the rock. Yet the turn is so sharp that if one paddles too hard and turns broadside, he is swamped in the white water. Although I did not make a perfect run I was not swamped. I paddled too hard on the right, the rock looming ominously, and I shipped water. But the run was over in less than a minute, which is a much, much shorter time than one usually has to wait before the verdict is announced.

We stopped for lunch on a sandy gravel beach, heating cans of chili in the fire; and we lay dozing afterward in the warm winter sun. In less than an hour after lunch we were out of the boxlike canyon; the walls were rolling gently back and opening up. Soon the river poured through the exit and we were on a broad, gravelly plain not far above Stillwell Crossing where Apache

Adams shortly came with a truck to pick us up with our gear and return us to his ranch house where we had left some cars.

The put-in point for Santa Elena is Lajitas (a very small town with a country store and filling station) which is about 12 miles upstream from the canyon proper on Highway 170 at the far western corner of the park.

It was in Lajitas that I saw skulls of Rio Grande catfish that had weighed up to 60 pounds. They were on display in a mesquite tree by the riverbank and the man who runs the nearby grocery store will take bets on the precise poundage of the fish who left these skulls behind.

Santa Elena usually takes two days not only because the put-in point is far above the canyon, but also because management of a famous rockslide—the Labyrinth—makes an overnight stop necessary. But for the rockslide the negotiation of the canyon would be almost idyllic, as the other rapids offer no great danger.

The drift down from the lazy site of Lajitas offers no particular challenge. Closer to the canyon, the river runs in loud but shallow rapids twisting left, then right; then it turns toward a spot in the hills where it seems completely to disappear under the mountain. There is indeed a sudden bend to the left and there is the yawning, vertical crack that marks the canyon. The water takes off downhill so fast one can see it falling; one's raft seems like a log in a roaring flume. As Hill wrote in the *Century* magazine, the flow of the water is "so silent as to be appalling." The lighted outside world disappears and the darkness of the canyon takes over. Sheer walls rise more than 1,000 feet straight up and the passage narrows to 50 feet or so. Santa Elena provides the most dramatic, breathtaking canyon entrance I know.

One has hardly become accustomed to it before real danger has arrived. For in less than a mile—probably a half-mile—the rockslide suddenly appears. The warning is a loud roar; the river turns left, and one is on the rockslide before he knows it. This slide is on the right or Mexican shore and on its upstream edge is a small sand bar. One has to paddle frantically for it in order to escape the maelstrom.

The slide is a tremendous jumble of boulders that reach up 250 feet or more on the Mexican side. This is not a loose talus slope of ordinary rocks. These rocks are larger than the houses we left to make this journey. The rocks are limestone, many of them being 35 feet high. Some are water polished and so slippery that they cannot be climbed but can be negotiated only by crawling under them. Others must be traversed. Somewhere on this slide an overnight camp must be made, for the daylight hours are almost gone. One can camp on the short upstream beach, cross the rockslide the next day with all his baggage, and then return for the boats. Or he can leave the boats safely tied to high rocks, carry his gear over the slide, camp on the lower side of the slide, and return in the morning to make the run in empty rafts. The latter is the preferable course, for loaded boats have no place in the powerful waters of the slide. Moreover, below the slide is an attractive, roomy camp site that gets some morning sun.

The slide demands the utmost respect. There are submerged boats in its angry waters. The river here pours under, as well as through, the gargantuan rock barrier; and the bodies of men are thought still to be caught somewhere under them.

The Hill party in 1899 carried their wooden boats over the great slide rather than risk the sluiceway.

Roy L. Swift of San Marcos has a letter from T. M. Meler, an old beaver trapper, who went through Santa Elena in 1905, a letter that Frank says is "a kind of classic of phonetic misspelling."

thirty years ago 3 of us wint throw the st. helena cannon rio grande river. wee bilt our bots about 300 miles up river from the cannon. wee were jest a bunch of old trapers which have traped all over the western pairt of texas & old mexico. I am not a riter jest a old traper. i traped the rio grande river that winter to brondvill, texas. i was on the river 3 month mecken the trip, wee weir trappen for bevers . . .

wee camped at the mounth [of Santa Elena] one nite. wee seen that thir had bin a u.s. pairtey wint throw the cannon about 5 yeairs before. theair dates was on the stones. [This was the first scientific exploration of the canyon led in 1899 by Dr. Robert T. Hill.] so we sed if uthers could go throw wee could do it too.

SO WEE STARTED in but when wee gott a bot a mile down the river wee come to a rock drift that was 2 or 300 feet hy and the river run under it. wee unloded our bots & started to packen over the drift [this was The Labyrinth]. this taken us 2 days to gitt our bots over. wee had to take rops & pull our bots over the top of that rock pile which was 300 feet abuve the water . . . the sides of the bluff [the cliffs] was about 2,000 feet hy on ether side.

we coulden see the son [sun] onley for about 2 ours ech day. well we had to go over some mitey ruff falls. we had to put ropes on our bots & warke them a round the age of those falls. I think theire was probley 8 or 10 of them . . . it was shore dark down in that hole but the wind shore blode throw their like a stove pipe.

[The trappers took four days "to get throw that hole" and lost one boat, two Winchester rifles, some traps, and most of their flour and coffee.]

thire isen iney liven thing in theair but huney beses, No fish no bevers no trees & not much lite. it ant much pleasher to go throw that cannon but lotes of hard work. i think that my trip throw it is my last trip.

But actually the waterway need not be too dangerous.

There is a "blind alley" terminating in a suck hole near the Texas side at the start of the main slide area. If, however, one lies in a rubber raft, keeping the center of gravity low, and stays to the right as he enters the main slide area, he can whirl through this sluiceway without serious danger or mishap. Those who sit high and try to negotiate the run with ordinary skills are apt to be in trouble.

In the winter of 1963 Bud Duncan of Killeen, Texas, tried to negotiate the slide with an aluminum boat on very high water. He was swept violently sideways into a crack between two large boulders, his boat, under the tremendous pressure of the river, bending into a U-shape. Duncan abandoned ship and managed to land on a rock downstream. Bob Burleson and Davis Bragg were next. They could not see from the starting point precisely what had happened. Their first news of impending disaster was when they rounded the bend and saw the jettisoned aluminum boat. Paddle as they did, they could not avoid it. The waters, sucking under the partial dam created by Duncan's boat, pulled their raft sideways like a giant vacuum cleaner, piling them up against it. Burleson and Bragg had to jump. Burleson reached a huge rock; Bragg was pulled into the suck hole and went under.

I asked Bob Burleson what went through his mind at that point.

"As I pulled myself up on the rock, I saw my waterproof matchbox case that I thought was safely in my pocket float away." With a grin on his face he added, "Up to then, I had been boasting to my friends that I had the only matchbox guaranteed to float in the Canyon."

Once Bragg submerged he had difficulty escaping entrapment. He told me he was down at least 20 feet and, at that level, gravel as big as grapefruit was hurtling through the water. Bragg came up twice under the rocks and each time was trapped. He despaired of escape, when the third time he bobbed to the surface. Davis, Duncan, and Burleson, each with a precarious perch on rocks, were finally rescued by other members of the party who, by throwing ropes, dragged them through dangerous waters to the sandy beach on the Mexican side.

I mentioned that as one approaches the slide the river turns left, strong paddling being necessary to land on the small sand bar. The truth is that in some seasons this small sand bar is not there. Jeff Bragg of Killeen, Texas, learned that to his sorrow. He and a friend were traveling in a rubber raft and counted on stopping at the sand bar around this turn in the river. But as they made the turn, they discovered that the sand bar had been washed out and they were sucked immediately into the maelstrom. They both survived, but miraculously so. The raft swamped. Jeff's companion was pulled under the water and trapped for a while under the rocks. Santa Elena is, indeed, a canyon to travel with the utmost respect.

The rest of the seven miles of the box canyon is a picnic. The walls are largely dark and they seem to come together at the top.

In this area I have the feeling of being shut in, of being in a close-fitting box, of being stifled. With some people that feeling is so acute they have traumatic reactions. I experienced no trauma—only a desire to hurry on, to put the canyon behind me. The matter is purely psychological, as one has ample room and no prospects of suffocation. Yet, there is a feeling of intimacy, of closeness. Although the walls are 50 feet or more apart, it seems as if one can touch each side at the same time. Their height and narrowness keep direct sunlight out most of the day and make the waterway below the great slide a truly mysterious canyon. The dark, silent, whirling water gives me a feeling of awe.

The exit is dramatic. This canyon does not slowly shrink; it maintains its height and grandeur to the very exit. I saw a bright shaft of sunlight ahead and in a few minutes I was in it, drenched with the cloudless brilliance of the Chihuahua Desert. The darkened cavern was far behind. The river was now so placid it was hard to imagine the energy it generated in the great slide.

The river spills quietly through the end of the canyon at a

place known as the Santa Elena Picnic Grounds. When I arrived, tourists with no idea of the dangers of Santa Elena were taking pictures of its mouth. Other friendly people were roasting a goat over an open fire and they invited us to join them. Their pit was near an ancient cottonwood, symbolic of Texas, as the Spanish word for the tree is Alamo. But neither Spanish nor English has words quite adequate to express either the beauty or the excitement of the canyons of the Rio Grande.

As I write these lines I think of Frank Desprez' poem "Lasca":

> And I wonder why I do not care
> For the things that are, like the
>   things that were.
> Does half my heart lie buried there
> In Texas, down by the Rio Grande?

These canyons of the Rio Grande are nevertheless hostile. There is treachery not so much in the sluiceways where the water is a gushing torrent as in the lesser riffles where snags of tree limbs lie under the surface. Jim Bowmer and the photographer, Bill Thompson (whom Bob Burleson characterized as the most casual of all boatmen since they both paddle on the same side at the same time), entered one such innocent-looking stretch only to have a six-inch hole torn in the bottom of their raft. Happily, Bob Burleson had sturdy patches and cement adequate to mend a hole of that size.

Fortunately, we had enough transportation so that, if necessary, we could have made room for those two boatmen in our other rafts. But those who venture the canyons alone in one raft take an awesome risk of a puncture that cannot be repaired, and that means either a long vigil while a rescue party works its way downriver or a hazardous, if not impossible, trek out on foot.

In many sections of these canyons the footpaths that lead to safety are nonexistent. It so happened, however, that even in the seemingly impassable Mariscal Canyon two Odessa college students, John Williams and Joe Hickey, miraculously escaped. Their rubber raft was punctured beyond repair. The boys spent two nights in the open in temperatures below 20°F. But the accident did not happen in the canyon proper but near the abandoned Johnson Ranch in the long approach to the canyon.

Moreover, any hike in these canyons is treacherous. Limestone weathers into sharp needlelike points that soon cut the stoutest shoes to pieces. Such was the experience of the Emory survey group in the 1850s; such is the experience today.

For those with extensive river experience these canyons offer only one other overwhelming risk and that is the risk of rising water—an experience I never had. Robert T. Hill knew that danger in 1899. Peter Koch of Alpine, Texas, who was with me in 1965, likewise once heard the ominous roar of a flood and saw an ugly wall of water coming down on him—what's known in Texas as a "gully washer." Taking to the river was the only sane decision. He was tossed like a chip on angry waters for miles. But it's the only way. And that risk is not ever-present. It is largely avoidable by following weather forecasts for it takes a big storm to put a new head on the languid Rio Grande.

I always leave the Rio Grande reluctantly. The swiftness of the rapids, the beauty of the canyon walls, the solitude of the chasm are too quickly passed. The urge is to return again and again in order to have a more intimate look, to explore the high caves, to search out the wealth of agates and fossils that these canyons reveal. It is hostile country in a sense, not even the water being safe to drink. The bushes mostly have spines; the walls are precipitous; the rocks are either dangerously brittle or dangerously sharp; the great slide in Santa Elena is terrifying. But the call of adventure is strong, and those who run these canyons once will return, drawn by the twin magnets of beauty and danger.

While I usually feel that the river is pulling me downhill at a tremendous speed, at times I feel I am moving uphill. Why, I am not sure. Perhaps it is the narrowing canyon. Perhaps it is when the rock strata slope downward.

I keep remembering what Frank X. Tolbert of the Dallas *Morning News* said about it. He was with us when we ran the Boquillas and told of the description of the country given more than 100 years ago by a Mexican vaquero:

"You go south from Fort Davis and, after a while, you come to a place where the rainbows wait for the rain, and the big river is kept in a stone box, and water runs uphill and the mountains float in the air, except at night when they go away to play with other mountains. . . ."

CHAPTER V

THE RIVER PEOPLE

West Texas is a hot, dry country that has few water holes. In 1860, Lieut. William H. Echols, with a pack train of 20 camels and 25 pack mules, made an extensive reconnaissance of it, looking for water and likely road locations. His outfit was composed of 31 men, exclusive of herders and camel attendants. He packed 500 gallons of water, each mule being rationed to two and a half gallons a day. In a little more than a week everyone was on short-water rations:

"The men have a quart of water issued tonight, and have enough for two drinks tomorrow, but they are so feeble and thirsty that it all would not last them an hour if they could get to it. The mules have stood it admirably, much to the wonder of everyone. All are in camp tonight, but cannot graze for their thirst. The camels are continually bellowing, which I suppose, as it is unusual, is a sign of a want of water."

This is one of our first accounts of the Chihuahua Desert whose fierce heat is reflected from the rocks in summer:

". . . a region in its original chaotic state, as if the progress of civilization was too rapid for the arrangement of chaos; a picture of barrenness and desolation, when the scathing fire of destruction has swept with its rabid flame mountains, canyons, ravines, precipices, cactus, soapweed, intense reflection from the limestone cliffs, and almost every barrier that one can conceive of to make an impossibility to progress."

This is why the early visitors, lacking equipment for deep-well drilling, gravitated to the river.

There are hot springs on the Rio Grande and some of them are in the park not far from the crossing to the Mexican village of Boquillas. Those hot springs were part of a homestead taken up by J. O. Langford in 1909. He was in poor health and came to this spot to try the medicinal waters. His wife and eighteen-month-old daughter were with him. They went overland by buckboard from Alpine through "strange and silent land that seemed to swallow us as quickly as the brush and grass had swallowed the quail," to quote from his book *Big Bend, A Homesteader's Story* (1955), p. 11.

Much of the expanse of land they covered was barren waste "where the alkali dust churned up by the burros and wagon wheels" almost choked them. It's a long distance between springs.

Langford's trip was not so difficult as Echols'; but it took ten days to make the journey from Alpine to Boquillas via McKinney, a distance of 180 miles. He built a house on the height of land overlooking the hot springs that are right on the edge of the Rio Grande at the mouth of Tornillo Creek. He made them a fair commercial success by erecting bathhouses and attracting patients from distant places to take the cure.

Today his bathhouses are gone, but the springs are fresh, clear, and warm, surrounded on three sides by thick stands of cane; and they attract many tourists. Langford trapped up and down the river, catching beaver, fox, opossum, skunk, and raccoon. Their *confreres* are still there, prowling the water front for food. He made friends with the river people—the Mexicans who work both sides of the river to eke out a bare subsistence.

When Langford came to this part of Big Bend, the grass was

high—so high and lush he thought it never could be eaten off. The grass provided sod that collected pools of rain water—little pools that lasted a few months and then became damp spots where greenness flourished. The land, though desertic in appearance, had life and subsistence values. Then came World War I, when prices of cattle, sheep, and goats soared. Eager for profits, the ranchers poured all the animals they could acquire into Big Bend. Cattle ate the prime grass. Sheep and goats were then brought in and they tore out the roots of what remained and pounded the earth to dust with their sharp hoofs. Grasslands were converted into bare, rain-eroded land. Bars of sun-baked sand and gravel took the place of pools and damp lands.

But the river life went on. The one who filled the void of Langford's absence was Maggie Smith, who died in 1965 at the age of sixty-nine. She used the stone store that Langford built— a place near the hot springs that is frequently inundated when the Rio Grande is in flood. That store, now vacant, still stands, and it is an enduring memorial to La Señora, as the river people called her. Maggie Smith slept with a six-shooter and a sawed-off shotgun. Once, when some rowdy cowboys stepped over the bounds of propriety, she beat them over the head with a wagon spoke. Another time she found a man looting her cash register.

"I put my thirty-eight between his shoulder blades and told him I was going to kill him," recalled Maggie. "I let him shiver and beg for a spell. He knew I was capable of letting him have it. Then I told him he could take off, and shot some around his heels and between his legs to hurry him on his way. He set a foot-race record that none of them Olympic varmints could match."

Maggie Smith was greatly loved. Her customers were mostly Mexicans who came from miles south of the border to trade with her. She did not always receive cash. Their credit was good and many accounts were long-standing. Maggie Smith was more than a merchant. She was also postmistress, for Hot Springs had a weekly delivery of mail by Ed Hancock out of Marathon. She was a friend of the river people, midwife, mother confessor, family counselor, banker, and undertaker. To *los pobres*—the poor ones—she was indeed La Señora, for it was to their needs that she catered. They often traded a goat or a pig for coffee and tobacco. Many of the Mexican children she helped bring into the world are called Maggie. One night a Mexican pounded on her door, wanting to sell a pig for $1.50. He needed the money to pay for the divorce of the woman he wanted to marry; and he admitted stealing the pig from the woman's husband. Maggie bought the pig for $1.50, adding $2.50 for a wedding license. Then she built a barbecue around the pig and invited all the interested parties to the feast.

Maggie Smith's main profit was in the wax that she bought from the Mexicans and resold to American processors. This wax is made from the candelilla plant. The wax business supports more than 20,000 people in northern Mexico. It is a monopoly of the Mexican government, which commands 90 per cent or more of the world market. Mexico licenses the gatherers of candelilla, allotting quotas to each family—100 kilos a year here, 150 kilos there, and so on. But it does not pay cash for the rough wax that the permittees deliver. Rather it gives chits, payable in six months. The poor Mexican, however, needs cash. So he's driven to collect candelilla beyond his quota and sell it in this country. He needs an export license from Mexico to do so law-fully, although we exact no duty. If he obtains this license, he may have to deal with a corrupt border official. So the Mexican, preferring to keep all the profit, seeks to avoid Mexican customs and sells directly to an American merchant.

Maggie Smith was such a merchant. She bought large quan-tities, selling them to refiners in Alpine or Marfa. Occasionally, the Mexican authorities obtained the help of our customs people

in policing the border. There would be raids; and Maggie, hearing the sound of approaching officials from the sensitive acoustical position of her store, would hide any wax in the ladies' rest room—a place that the border officials, being gentlemen, never entered. But a crisis developed when large quantities of wax were stolen in Mexico and smuggled across the border. Both countries agreed that the border should be sealed; and it was—for a while. The sealing, however, put such a pinch on Maggie Smith's business that she liquidated it. She moved to an inholding at San Vicente a few miles up the river for a couple of years, staying there until the land was acquired by the Park Service. Then she went to nearby Boquillas, Mexico, and later to Lajitas, far to the west, on the United States side of the river. When she left Hot Springs, her accounts receivable were $12,000. How much she collected we do not know. But it is thought that most of it went uncollected.

She spent the last years of her life running the store at Study Butte (pronounced Stoody), a few miles inland.

Another kindhearted merchant at Hot Springs was Peter Koch. He moved there with his wife, Etta, in 1945 to give her a mild winter climate. They stayed until spring only to return ten years later (1955), after Maggie Smith's departure, to run the Trading Post for a year. Peter, like Maggie, was a friend of the river people; knowing their weakness, he came to their protection; knowing their basic integrity, he spoke up in their defense. The river people never had stouter friends than Maggie Smith and Peter Koch.

Study Butte—where Maggie died—is near Terlingua on the park's edge—a word which is a corruption of the Spanish "The Land Speaks."

Terlingua has long been the most important point in the Big Bend country for the river people. They shopped there and found much work there. Up to World War II Terlingua was the cinnabar or mercuric sulphide capital of the world. The mines are operated occasionally, but the town has the appearance of a ghost city. There is no blade of grass. The large adobe house occupied by the owner of the mine has lost its doors and window-panes. The adobe houses of the workers, once a bright yellow, now show but a wall or two and sometimes can be identified only by piles of rubble marking their sites. One long adobe building, with a porch running its full length, is intact. Nearby at the old Terlingua Creek crossing is a post office, a general store, and a school for a dozen or more children.

Terlingua today is possessed mostly by lizards. There is no touch of greenery, even in the graveyard marked by rough rock headstones and hand-hewn crosses. Terlingua, sun baked and desolate, seems even more lonely with the passing of Maggie Smith— ambassador of good will along the Rio Grande.

On Maggie Smith's death Terlingua had 16 residents. Among these was an elderly lady who had a pet black goat and a hard-drinking son who ran the Chisos Oasis—a beer joint and agate rock shop. She had a good ranch in the hill country, but she moved to Terlingua because her son, although arrested elsewhere, had immunity in Terlingua. "Down here they just don't give a damn what Smokey does."

The post office at Terlingua does a brisk business. It is quicker for Mexicans across the river to get a letter to interior Mexico via Terlingua than through the Mexican postal service. But Terlingua is so small, according to Bob Murphy of Nacogdoches, it "doesn't even have a village idiot."

Maggie Smith told about Terlingua's voting record in the 1964 election. She said Goldwater did not concede until the returns from Terlingua were in. Terlingua cast 16 ballots and all were for Johnson!

Terlingua is known as the "Chili Capital of the World"—so named by Frank X. Tolbert of the Dallas *Morning News*. It is incorporated. And more or less as a joke it acquired a distinguished list of officials:

MAYOR	David A. Witts
WATER COMMISSIONER	Frank X. Tolbert
PARK COMMISSIONER	John B. King
CITY METEOROLOGIST	James Underwood
AIRPORT MANAGER	George Haddaway
ROAD COMMISSIONER	Murray Forsvall
SOCIAL DIRECTOR	Carroll Shelby
CHIEF JUSTICE, MUNICIPAL COURT	Thomas J. Tierney
DIRECTOR MUSEUM OF MODERN ART	B. R. Neale
DIRECTOR OF LIBRARIES	Holland McCombs
SUPERINTENDENT OF SCHOOLS	William T. Rives

Mr. Shelby developed the Cobra sports car for Ford and races under the decal of Terlingua Racing Team, showing an angry jack rabbit against a field of bright orange and yellow. And the magazine, *Sports Car Graphic,* has been seriously promoting a sports car race in and around Terlingua. The promoters recently got out an advertisement of Terlingua. (See page 100.)

The people who frequent Terlingua, who engage in the wax-reducing business, and who live along the Rio Grande, are commonly referred to as Mexicans. They still come to this country as "wet-backs" looking for cotton to pick or cattle to herd. They are excellent laborers, and employers along our border welcome them. They are steady workers and good family men. They send their families in the interior of Mexico 95 per cent of their pay checks. And even when our Department of Labor bars them, they draw on their cunning to come furtively, but peacefully, looking for work. Their deportment is a credit to any border.

Their language is what Frank X. Tolbert calls Tex-Mex, illus-

TERLINGUA, TEXAS:
"Your Convention City"

Hold Your 1965 Convention in Terlingua...

THE FASTEST GROWING CITY ON DIRTY WOMEN CREEK

Terlingua is the undisputed "chili capital of the world." SEE THE GIGANTIC STATUE OF WICK FOWLER . . . Life Size.

30,000 ACRES OF FREE PARKING

Have fun in Terlingua: Don't worry about the cops; no police force, and the chief justice lives in Dallas...

TERLINGUA, TEXAS:
"Your Convention City"

FACILITIES WHICH TERLINGUA HAS Not: MAGNIFICENT HOTELS, THEATRES, RESTAURANTS, NIGHTCLUBS, PEOPLE.

"Terlingua is a fun town. We had our 1964 convention in Terlingua and plan to come back in '65." Dr. Victor Frisbie, president of the Tex-Mex Marihuana and Candililla Smugglers Association.

"WELCOME TO TERLINGUA," DAVID A. WITTS, MAYOR; FRANK X. TOLBERT, WATER COMMISSION; JOHN E. KING, PARK COMMISSIONER; CARROLL SHELBY, SOCIAL DIRECTOR; THOMAS JEFFERSON TIERNEY, CHIEF JUSTICE AND "THE LAW WEST OF DIRTY WOMEN CREEK"; BILL NEALE, DIRECTOR, MUSEUM OF MODERN ART; WILLIAM T. RIVES, SCHOOL SUPT. AND POET LAUREATE; HOLLAND McCOMBS, LIBRARIAN; JIM UNDERWOOD, CITY METEOROLOGIST; JOE MASHMAN, CHIEF DOG CATCHER; CHEVUS CHAPMAN, CITY TREASURER AND ASSISTANT DOG CATCHER; PAUL CRUME, DIRECTOR OF MONUMENTS; COL. IRVING HARRIGAN, DIRECTOR OF CITY SANITATON DEPARTMENT BAND.

trated by a version of "The Night before Christmas" distributed by Bill (Don Pedro) Rudd of Brownsville:

'Tis the night before Christmas and all through the casa
Not a creature is stirring: Caramba, Que pasa?
The stockings are hanging con mucho cuidado
In hopes that Saint Nicholas will feel obligado
To leave a few cosas aqui and alli

For chico y chia (y something for me).
Los ninos are snuggled all safe in their camas
Some in vestidos and some in pajamas.
Their little cabezas all full of good things.
They're all esperando que Santa will bring.
SANTA ESTA at the corner saloon
Muy borracho since mid-afternoon.
Mama is sitting beside la ventana
Shining her rolling pin para manana.
When Santa returns to his home zigzaguendo,
Lit up like the Star-Spangled Banner, contando.
And Mama will send him to bed con a right
Merry Christmas a todos, y a todos good night!

The river people, however, are not of pure Spanish blood. Mixed with it is Indian blood. Today all the Indians are gone, their extermination being described by Newcomb in *The Indians of Texas* (1961). Many were hunted down and killed; many died of disease. The rest were absorbed over the centuries by the Mexicans.

The earliest Indians are often called Basket Makers, but the archaeologists prefer the name Desert Culture Type. They occupied the Big Bend country until about the fourteenth century.

During the early centuries these Indians lacked knowledge of the bow and arrow. Their homes were in caves in canyon walls. The midden shows fish bones and the bones of animals, including deer. Shells of clams and of snails fill some of the debris. A few bones of the now-extinct bison are found. Apparently some corn was used in later times. Great quantities of buckeye, mesquite, laurel, and the small western walnut, which still grows in part of the area, have been dug up.

Specimens of their work include wooden implements, beads, and gourds.

Ropes were made; mats and baskets woven; nets for catching rabbits (some nets 200 feet long) fashioned. The fiber used came from a variety of plants which when beaten to a pulp gave up their sinews. These early Indians made no pottery, but they wove blankets and twilled matting. They wore sandals of woven yucca leaves.

They used awls made by sharpening bones of animals. They had no shuttles, all weaving apparently being done tediously by hand. They made pouches of animal skins. They cut rabbit skin into long strips and wound the strips around cords. Then they wove the cords together, making a warm rabbit-skin blanket. Their weapons were the dart thrower (atlatl) and a curved throwing club; and their knives and dart points were flint.

The Indian civilization did not stand still. In time these Indians learned how to make pottery; and in time they got the bow and arrow. Whether they worked these discoveries out themselves or learned from neighbors is much mooted.

Although much archaeological work remains to be done, its prospects do not seem bright. For legends and tales were long common describing vast quantities of gold which the early Spanish explorers were supposed to have cached in the mountains. This prompted many to clear out the accumulated debris of caves and incidentally destroy whatever archaeological material might be present. Moreover, as we shall see, dams are covering up some precious sites; and as this is written, archaeologists and paleontologists are working overtime on so-called "salvage" assignments to preserve whatever is possible before the impounded waters bury these sites forever.

The Desert Indians were overrun by the Apaches and Comanches about the fourteenth century. The Apaches and Comanches, unlike the Desert Indians, did not occupy the Big Bend. They were transients who worked hard to find food and sustenance in this desert wilderness. They also used Big Bend as a route to Mexico, where they raided and pillaged. The park entrance road, indeed, closely follows the historic Comanche Trail. The

Indians followed the food supply, coming south in the spring and gathering the fruits of this desert. They also planted corn, beans, and melons along the Rio Grande. They hunted and fished and, under the adversity of this harsh regime, they developed cunning and cleverness and the knack of survival. They found flint and agates and exploited them for points for darts and later for arrows. Some of the sites where they turned this flaky rock into instruments of destruction can be visited today by those who travel by jeep and on foot. Each of the habitats was near a spring and had carefully arranged exits. Each was located with an eye against surprise attack.

The Indians never perished from thirst or hunger in the desert—not when they carried knives. For with a knife a cactus can be opened.

Any cactus with a milky sap is poisonous to man. But the rest are not. The Indians relied on cacti of the round species, inserting a knife into the side near the top and making a horizontal cut around it. The top was lifted off and chunks of the center were cut out and chewed. The juice quenches the thirst and has some food value; but the pulp is chewed only, not eaten.

The fruit of the prickly pear was eaten. Both ends were sliced off and the skin slit lengthwise. It peels back easily and you have a delicious red pulp or yellow pulp, according to the variety.

The Indians planted them for food. The Franciscan monks planted them around their missions, partly for food and partly as a protective hedge. Some Mexican people use the tender young pads, which they call *los nopalitos*, for food. They scrape off the spines with a knife and roast the pads or cut them into strips and boil or fry them. They may be dipped in butter and cooked in a deep fat or sizzled in their own juice and then folded in a tortilla and covered with chili sauce. The small pads, too, may be cut in small squares and canned for use like any other green vegetable.

The Indians took the young leaves of the prickly pear and boiled them.

They made jelly—as people still do—from the fruit of the prickly pear.

The Indians used the fruit of the prickly pear as a cure for rheumatism. They cut the fruit open and laid the pulp side against the affected part of the body. They also placed it on the head to stop a headache.

The juice of the plant, which is like glue, was used for dyes.

They took the stalk of the yucca where the basal leaves sprout and cut out chunks for chewing. The pulp is sweet, and cattle as well as man enjoy it. A good deal of the leisure time of the Indians was evidently spent in chewing these chunks of yucca. Prolonged chewing was apparently required, the end product being a quid composed of nothing but the fiber of the plant.

The Indians took the cabbagelike base of the sotol and baked it. The river people still find it delicious. The Indians also fermented it and made a fiery drink called sotol. The river people do the same. The Indians often baked the young stalk of the century plant with the sotol or turned it into a liquor. The river people still do.

The Indians ate the blossoms of the yucca.

They boiled the pods of the mesquite for food.

The strawberry cactus has a delicious fruit that man has eaten from the earliest time.

The agaves or century plants were used for soap, for medicine, and for fibers.

The Indians took rattlesnakes and rendered the oil and grease, which they rubbed into their joints when they had rheumatism or sore muscles.

They boiled large quantities of greasewood and made a hot brew and in this brew soaked arthritic joints.

They also boiled the lechuguilla to make a brew for rheumatic ailments, a brew which recently has been discovered to contain a definite amount of cortisone.

They used the sagebrush to make a brew for the treatment of diabetes.

The road runner or *paisano* was wrapped in clay, baked in hot ashes, and then eaten as a blood tonic.

A sunflower brew was used in the case of sunstroke.

Charcoal from mesquite wood was a remedy for dysentery.

The bleached horns of deer were ground up to make a powder and this powder was mixed with the fresh, warm blood of a deer as a potion for the cure of heart conditions.

The brew of kidney seed was used for jaundice.

A brew made from the tarbush was used as a laxative.

Sunflower seeds were used to make a poultice for sprained ankles or wrists.

Illness, such as headaches and rheumatism, was also treated by a medicine man with a tube made out of a rock. The doctor would press the tube against the skin at a place where the symptoms were felt and go through the motions of sucking on the tube. The ritual was apparently of long duration, ending with the medicine man producing a wad of foreign matter which he ostensibly had drawn from the sick person's body. And the legend is that the patient the next day invariably felt better.

The Indians of West Texas were unruly and lawless. They stole, murdered, and plundered rival tribes and the white settlers, too. But the more one travels the Big Bend the more he admires their cunning, skill, and endurance. They lived and even flourished in a harsh, cruel environment that would have destroyed others.

They, like the golden eagle, were conservationists. They knew that, if they took too much this year or stayed too long in one place, they would ruin it for another year. And so they kept moving. They were like Walker, the notorious horse thief, who arrived on the scene much later and ran off all the livestock but never molested a settler.

"Bless your hearts," he is reported as saying. "I'd never harm a hair of any of you. I want you to live and prosper so that another year you'll have more livestock for me to rustle."

What I have said so far about the Indians of West Texas has telescoped many centuries, drawing no clear distinction between them. Although the over-all knowledge is skimpy, discerning students, such as E. Mott Davis and David S. Dibble of the University of Texas, Donald J. Lehmer of the University of Omaha, Mr. and Mrs. C. B. Cosgrove of the Peabody Museum, and Alex D. Krieger of the University of Washington, have done much to separate the various epochs and to plot through studies of projectile points and other artifacts the evolutionary flow of the culture.

Some of the most promising sites will be buried by the reservoir behind Amistad Dam on the Rio Grande—a concrete dam with earthen wings not far upstream from Del Rio, Texas, and right below the confluence of sparkling Devil's River and the muddy Rio Grande. It will back water some 86 miles up the Rio Grande and flood areas of the Devil's and Pecos Rivers.

Devil's River is spring fed and never goes dry, although its tributary, Dry Devil's Run, carries only surface runoffs.

Over at Corpus Christi, Cyrus Tilloson, veteran post officer, gives the following legend concerning the way in which the river got its name. It seems that Captain Rip Ford of the Texas Rangers was headed west on the trail of some Comanches. He came across this stream during the time of the rains when it was in flood. His Mexican guide called it Rio San Pedro. "Saint's River, hell!" snorted Rip Ford. "More like the Devil's!" And that name, according to Cyrus Tilloson, stuck.

The low hills south of Comstock, through which Devil's River flows, have symmetrical contour lines looking from the air as if they had been disked. Those contours are made up of thin layers of limestone rock, a good producer of water in this parched land. Goodenough Springs—which is about a quarter-mile from the

Rio Grande—boils out of a pit lined on three sides by 30-foot cliffs. It is a kidney-shaped pool about 30 feet wide that serves as a watering place for occasional livestock in this sun-baked, desiccated region. Goodenough is the third largest spring in Texas, ranking only below Comal and San Marcos, which I discuss in a later chapter. Between 1960 and 1965 it flowed as high as 156 and not less than 102 cubic feet per second. Its water is clear and cold and it runs into the Rio Grande a short distance to the south. Nearby, the Devil's River winds its serpentine way for some miles through dry, thirsty land that is baked in sunshine most of the year and dotted by scrub. But it has enough water to maintain two hydroelectric plants—one at Devil's Lake and one at Lake Walk—both of which will be inundated by the waters of Amistad Dam.

The reservoir behind the dam (constructed by the International Boundary and Water Commission pursuant to a treaty between the United States and Mexico) will be filled by June, 1968.

At least 300 *recorded* sites on the Texas side of the Rio Grande or its tributaries and at least 68 on the Mexican side will be flooded or destroyed. Richard Ambler, director of the Texas Archaeological Salvage Project in Austin, says that when probable sites are added to recorded sites there will be somewhere in the vicinity of 700 destroyed or flooded.

One is on Devil's River near the dam, explored by LeRoy Johnson, Jr., of the University of Texas and described in his brochure, *The Devil's Mouth Site* (1964). There, a long sequence of Indian occupations dating from 6000 B.C. to A.D. 1000 has been defined.

I visited another farther west, one located on the Pecos not far from its confluence with the Rio Grande. U.S. Route 90 west of Del Rio crosses the Pecos on Texas' highest bridge. At the eastern edge of that bridge is an overlook with a splendid view of the gorge of the Pecos. Downstream from the bridge and on the west side of the river are cliffs, visible from the overlook, where rich findings have been made by Dr. David S. Dibble. We crossed the bridge over the Pecos and took a sharp right to follow the old road that runs under the present bridge. In half a mile or so we reached the site, then being worked by Dr. Dibble and four staff members.

This is a semi-arid, hilly region where the altitude does not exceed 1,500 feet and the rainfall is about 16 inches a year. Limestone forms the country rock and it has been sharply eroded into deep gorges. There are many watercourses in the region. But most of them are dry and carry water only during periods of rain. Flash floods have long caused the Pecos to rise angrily and flood its high banks and shoulders. Thorny shrubs and cacti dominate the scene. On our arrival young mesquite looked freshly leafed out, although this was January. The castor bean was in pod. The alluvial deposits of the Pecos were churned up into a fine dust as we walked. The temperature that reaches as high as 110°F. in the summer was a pleasant 60 degrees this winter day.

Dr. Dibble was excavating the first 25 feet of a wall that had all but filled in a cave whose roof was at one time a wide limestone overhang. On the ground level campfires and camp-site debris had made a stratum a foot or so deep. Then the river had deposited a layer of alluvial soil on the top of that layer. The next layer was midden from other camps and so on, alternately, to a point about three feet beneath the limestone overhang.

Each level was being combed and sifted for artifacts, shovelful by shovelful. The levels that made up the 20-odd feet of midden and alluvial deposits probably represented a span of 8,000 years. The top thin layer, representing perhaps the last century of occupation, showed tobacco cans. Lower layers revealed early man. Much of the debris was made up of coarse limestone gravel, which is the product of hundreds of campfires. Early man in this hemisphere had no pottery. Pottery did not arrive in West Texas until 300 to 200 B.C. Early man did his cooking on flat rocks heated in the fire. As large, flat limestone rocks of the Pecos were used again and again, they cracked and fragmented under heat, their gravel being moved aside to make room for other large rocks. And so it is that caves, with telltale talus slopes of limestone rock, mark sites used by early man for his home. The talus slopes spewing out of this cave on the Pecos were 20 feet or more in length.

Many mussel shells were in the site; and there were bones apparently used for necklaces. Projectile points for darts were present, the bow and arrow not being invented until about A.D. 600 to 800.

In the diggings that I visited on the Pecos were enough bones to indicate that these early Indians were meat and fish eaters. Mortars made of limestone were also common, and a few pestles. But this does not necessarily indicate that they were farmers. Agriculture, indeed, probably did not come in until about 2000 B.C. The mortars were probably used only to grind seeds which are common in the area: cactus seeds, pods of the mesquite and acacia, castor-bean seeds, piñon nuts, acorns, walnuts, sunflower seeds, hackberries, buckeyes, and nuts from an occasional pistachio tree.

This limestone cliff was so fascinating and the quiet and solitude of the gorge so profound, that I wanted to tarry until sundown. But time pressed as we still had a few stops to make before dark. One was on Mile Creek which empties into the Rio Grande at Langtry, Texas. Dr. Dibble escorted us there with a sense of excitement, for it was on Mile Creek that he had personally made a notable discovery.

Langtry is the home of the late Judge Roy Bean, immortalized in *The Law West of the Pecos,* who pronounced some memorable dicta: "If a man is standing still, he's not carrying a pistol. If he is moving, he is traveling and has a right to carry it."

Judge Bean's old establishment has been well preserved and maintained as a tourist attraction. But the name Jersey Lily Saloon no longer appears on it. A group of citizens, more interested in reform than in history, removed that sign and replaced it with a tamer one, Billiard Hall—a sport unknown to Langtry in the rough-and-ready days of Judge Bean. Langtry is a friendly, wind-swept town that sits under the skimpy shade of mesquite trees. Guy Skiles, Langtry's leading citizen, is an Indian student in his own right, having explored dozens of caves and made collections of artifacts, some of which he presented to museums, some of which he has on display. We pored over them as Mrs. Skiles served us piping-hot coffee. Then he took us to the Mile Creek bluff, near which his house stands, from which we viewed the deep, dry arroyo washed out by centuries of flash floods. At its mouth on the Mexican side of the Rio Grande is a flat green pasture several acres in size.

"It was there," Skiles said, "that Fitzsimmons and Maher fought on February 21, 1896." The fight had been scheduled for Dallas, but a special session of the Texas legislature made it a felony to hold a prize fight in Texas. The promoter moved the fight to El Paso. But the Texas Rangers were ordered to stop it. Roy Bean invited the fighters to Langtry, and wired San Antonio for a carload of beer. He made a pontoon bridge by lashing boats together. The crowd used the bridge to cross to Mexico for the fight and then returned to Langtry to buy beer from the man "who knew good business when he saw it."

But to get back to Mile Creek and its archaeological treasures. Mile Creek is now famous for Dibble's work. His book, *Bonfire Shelter,* tells an exciting story of early man who once frequented this gorge. We visited the site, scrambling down a precipitous limestone cliff, skirting mesquite, willow, and cottonwoods, hiking a stretch of canyon whose floor was huge polished slabs interspersed with patches of coarse sand, and then climbing the opposite side and entering near the top a high-vaulted overhang.

This overhang seldom sees direct sunlight. It is long and spacious, offering elbow room for dozens of people. It was here that Dibble dug and made exciting discoveries, one of which was artifacts traced, through carbon-14 tests, to 10,250 years ago.

At that time a bison (*B. antiquus*), ancestor of our modern buffalo and about one-third larger, occupied this part of West Texas. The early Indians hunted it, one of the favorite methods being to stampede the herds, driving them over the 100-foot cliff of Mile Creek that borders this shelter where Dibble did his digging.

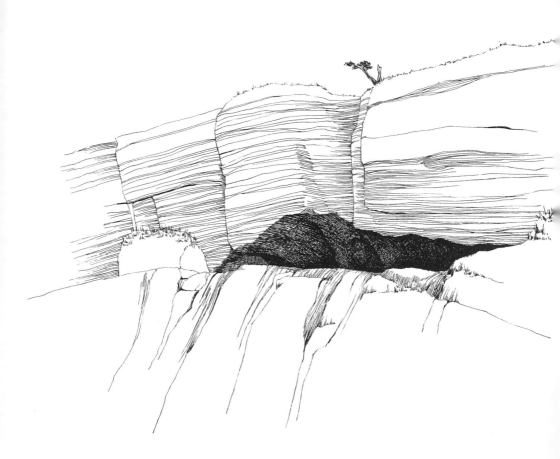

Dibble found thick deposits of the bones of this early bison. Above these deposits were layers of bones of the modern buffalo. Seven thousand years had passed since the early bison had been slaughtered. Now it was about 1000 B.C. and the modern buffalo had appeared on the scene. At least 1,000 of them were killed here. One young buffalo carcass was still intact. The other bones had packed down into tight strata and apparently had burned from spontaneous combustion. No tail bones were recovered, Dr. Dibble believing that, since "the tail goes with the hide," the animals were skinned and the hides used for some purpose. A now extinct horse, a camel, and an elephant were also found at Bonfire Shelter.

Dibble found many projectile points both with the ancient bison bones and with the later ones. With the former were dart points known as Plainview, named for the town of Plainview in Hale County, north of Lubbock, where this kind of point was first found associated with the extinct bison.

Dibble found a Folsom projectile point along with the Plainview points. That artifact is named for Folsom, New Mexico, where J. D. Figgins of the Denver Museum of Natural History found this fluted specimen in 1927 between the ribs of an extinct bison. The Folsom point is unique:

> Another arresting feature was the shape of the point—unique in all the history of primitive man—and the fact that it was better made than any other point of equal antiquity. It was rather broad, with a deep concave base that terminated at each side in a jutting point, or "ear." The edges were most skillfully chipped, and the base and ears were often ground smooth. It was particularly distinguished by the fact that a long flake of stone had been chipped away on each face from the base almost to the tip. The flute, or channel, left by the flake, made the point look a little like the end of a grooved bayonet. This is the true or classic Folsom.—Macgowen and Hester, *Early Man in the New World* (Natural History Library, 1962 ed.), p. 148.

Dibble explained that the Rio Grande Indians may not have made this particular point, that it may have been imported. Guy Skiles, the amateur paleontologist of Langtry, Texas, had a similar view.

"I reckon," he told me, "that a bison brought this in from the north—between his ribs or imbedded in his hindquarters."

No one will ever know. But the bison bones, the Plainview points, the Folsom point, and carbon-14 studies take the Indians of the Rio Grande back about 10,250 years.

I left these diggings with sadness. The location of each had a sublime atmosphere. Each is a quiet, secluded spot for reflection and repose. I came to understand the zeal and drive of the archaeologist who sifts through the site looking for artifacts. His thrill is that of a detective putting clues together, not to re-enact an episode but to reconstruct a whole society. Who were these early Indians? What were their fears, their joys, their wants, their needs? Who was their God? What were their spiritual ties with the universe? What was their music like? Their love songs?

Archaeology has not been our forte. We have treated it in a niggardly way. Only when disaster threatens do we become generous with funds for archaeologists. Once a dam is scheduled, archaeological salvage operations get under way. By then, time is short, the scientist having only a few months, where he needs years, to do a thorough study.

In Austin I was talking with Prof. E. Mott Davis about this condition. I told him about TVA's plan to put a dam across the Little Tennessee River, destroying forever one of the loveliest rivers and one of the prettiest valleys God ever created.

"The only ardent TVA supporter I could find was an archaeologist."

"Because TVA would finance digging on a salvage basis?"

"Exactly."

Professor Davis laughed as he said, "Don't misjudge us archeologists. We're not as destructive of natural beauty as our enthusiasm for salvage projects might indicate."

Becoming reflective, he added:

"There have been Texans for at least 12,000 years, but we hear less about them than about Cro-Magnon or Neanderthal man because they have been little studied compared to those much-investigated foreigners.

"Unfortunately, the evidences of prehistory do not last forever, and one of the prices of modern civilization is that the march of progress is destroying the record of the past. In Texas, construction of highways and reservoirs, urban expansion, and indiscriminate relic hunting are taking a remarkably high toll of archaeological sites every year."

There are less than twenty professional archaeologists in Texas and they are racing against the clock of so-called "progress" to salvage what may be in the most promising sites.

"This loss of sites," Professor Davis told me, "sometimes represents the permanent disappearance of whole sections of the human record."

Thanks to the late Forrest Kirkland, the Pecos River pictographs will not be lost. He was a Dallas artist who by chance heard of some Indian rock paintings on a cliff along the Concho River near the town of Paint Rock, east of San Angelo. He and his wife investigated, and what he discovered consumed the remaining years of his life. On rock walls under overhanging ledges, where the Indians had camped from time out of mind, were hundreds of paintings in color. About a fourth of them had been destroyed by vandals. So he decided to copy them in water colors. He also included in his project the pictographs at Meyer's Springs near Dryden in Terrell County, those at Fort Davis and at Hueco Tanks near El Paso—indeed, all the known pictograph sites in Texas. Among the most interesting were those in the lower Pecos River region. They have all been reproduced by Kirkland in water colors, each being a scale replica and the colors being as faithful a reproduction of the Indian hues as possible. They have now been published by the University of Texas Press in a volume edited by our Indian authority, W. W. Newcomb.

Little is known about the Indians that made these pictographs. They were neither midgets nor giants. They were apparently small in stature. But their customs and their societal structure are largely unknown. As Dr. Newcomb has said, these pictographs are "enigmatic artistic efforts of a mysterious people, suspended in the void of our ignorance."

Herds of deer, pierced by darts, are shown. Cougars are crouching or leaping. Strange masked human figures are there. Some have medicine bags attached to their arms. Geometric designs appear. A huge snake is much in evidence. Handprints are shown. Dancing figures are on display. While most of the pictographs are painted in red, orange, or black, some are in crayon. Newcomb has ventured the opinion that the masked figures were probably shaman or medicine men. When depicted throwing darts at game, a religious ceremony was being depicted. For the act of painting was a magical attempt to ensure success in the chase. But what the other worries and concerns of these people, reduced to pictorial form (including one of a giant comb), may have been we do not yet know. But thanks to Kirkland, the pictorial record has been preserved— "a large collection of faithfully rendered masterpieces unequaled and unparalleled." To quote again from Newcomb, "That the sun-scorched shelters of the Pecos and other remote, dusty cliff walls scattered across Texas could support a sophisticated and attractive art form seems at first ludicrous; nonetheless, it is true."

On my Texas journey I found other dams that either have destroyed or will destroy hundreds of archaeological sites. Stillhouse Hollow Dam on the Lampasas River in Bell County—one of the richest archaeological counties in the state that had some 1500 Indian camp sites—will flood 100 known archaeological sites plus many not yet fully recorded. Nearby is Belton Dam which wiped out several hundred sites; and the proposed elevation of that dam by another 25 feet will flood 50 to 75 more of the presently recorded sites. These include some of the most colorful ones I have seen, located on Kell Branch.

Texas has under way several hundred minor dams and watershed projects, which will be highly destructive, archaeologically speaking. There are, in addition, 10 new major reservoir projects that will impose the death sentence on hundreds of other unexplored archaeological sites.

The archaeologists are breathless, working on the run. The Texas Archaeological Salvage Project is working on sites that will be inundated by 15 major reservoir projects. Southern Methodist University's Department of Anthropology is working on sites behind three others.

These, however, are only tiny portions of a few selected sites in each flood pool. Funds for archaeological work are short and when the money runs out, digging must stop, even if the archaeologist is within a few feet or a few weeks of a major contribution.

Dams, dams, dams—they are the plague of Texas. They are a modern form of pork-barrel grants. Other sources of power are plentiful. When dams are needed for flood control, they could be placed high on the tributaries. They not only silt in early and become useless; they often produce ugly shore lines of mud and debris; they destroy forever rich bottom lands; and they are wiping out the chronicles of early man that give Texas some of its richest culture.

The dam builders are among the most destructive Ahabs that Texas knows.

CHAPTER VI

THE DAVIS MOUNTAINS

The Davis Mountains that stand in splendor across the Chihuahua Desert north of the Chisos have a greater rainfall than the plains and ridges to the south. They contain as good grasslands as any in the Southwest; and water is plentiful, if not abundant. The rich grama grasses are present. Idaho fescue is abundant along with muhly, barnyard grass, the brome grasses, June grass, and wheat grass—all good forage.

These nutritious grasses are the basis of vast cattle empires. The grasses cure on the stalk, and cattle and horses fatten on them. In the Davis Mountains some one and a half million acres are used as grazing lands by 100 ranchers. Some of these ranches are run by conservation-minded men, such as Don McIvor and E. R. Eppenauer. Some of the ranches have odd names: U Up and U Down, o6, o3, o2—each describing a particular registered brand of which each ranch has several. Lightning Ranch near Marathon uses two slashes of lightning (⟍) on the left shoulder as its brand. The Joe Lane Ranch of Alpine uses the Quien Sabe (Don't Know) brand (⌢). The Kokernot Ranch near Alpine uses o6 as its brand and follows the custom in selling cattle to provide that, apart from packer cattle, they must be shipped outside Texas. But brand names are dying out, partly because branding is somewhat disappearing due to fencing and the elimination of the open range, partly because brands reduce the value of the hide and add an operational cost, partly because the use of brand names makes the cattle ranch, to the owner's disgust, sound like a dude ranch.

The Davis Mountains contain the finest grasslands in West Texas. As one moves south toward the Chisos the grasses are more and more mixed with cactus, sotol, and agave. The mixed area provides browse for deer; and cattle also take some of it. Some of the early cattlemen—Alfred Gage, for example—preferred the mixed area over the pure grasslands, as it gave additional assurance of feed in case of severe drought. And this land has always been plagued by that threat. The farther south one goes the poorer the land and the thinner the grass. Davis Mountain land is indeed richer in soil than that of the Chisos. The tendency over the years has been to put more stock on the land than it will bear. Overgrazing exacts a heavy toll, for the rains come in downpours, as much as three inches falling in 15 minutes. If overgrazing has started, erosion takes place quickly and disastrously. The 20 inches of rain distributed equally over the year would be only a boon and a blessing. But coming quickly, as it often does, flash floods are produced; and the runoffs take the thin overlay of humus that it took thousands of years to produce. So long as conservation is practiced and there is no overgrazing, the minerals are preserved and the grasses remain nutritious. Once erosion starts, the land begins a downward cycle that ends in the creation of a desert. That has happened in most of the land on the fringes of the Davis Mountains and it is happening in large areas in the mountains proper.

The Davis Mountains, now famous for grazing, were early associated with our military undertakings in West Texas.

Fort Davis—established in 1854 and abandoned in 1891—

was located first in a box canyon near Limpia Creek in the Davis Mountains and then at the mouth of the canyon. Today the remains of Fort Davis are a National Historic Site located on Route 17 not far north from Marfa. The history of Fort Davis is a vital chapter in our chronicles. Texas joined the Union on the eve of the Mexican War (1846–1848), a war which added New Mexico, Arizona, and California to the United States. Prospects for this new territory brightened with the discovery of gold in California in 1849. Since the central routes were marked by massive mountains and deep snows, the southern routes became attractive. A vital unit of one southern route was the road from San Antonio to El Paso. It was along that road that hundreds of immigrants and dozens of freight trains traveled West beginning in 1849.

The Spanish spent nearly 300 years trying to conquer and colonize this region. The Mexicans next had their turn and failed. The year 1850 marked the beginning of the American epoch.

In 1847 regular U.S. mail service to the Pacific Coast via vessels and the Isthmus of Panama had been inaugurated. Overland mail service to the intermountain region was begun in 1850. In that year the San Antonio–El Paso link was welded, Henry Skillman carrying the first mail. Only daylight runs were made, and it took 30 days to cover the distance of 673 miles. As a result, only one mail a week, each way, was delivered.

Stagecoach traffic started in the Southwest in 1853, when George H. Giddings was awarded a Federal mail contract on the San Antonio–El Paso road. He was followed by James Buck, who in turn was succeeded by the famous Butterfield Overland Mail.

Under the Act of March 3, 1857 (11 Stat. 190), the bid for overland mail, submitted by John Butterfield and his group, starting at St. Louis and going via El Paso for a distance of nearly 2,800 miles, was accepted. Wells had to be sunk and reservoirs

made to assure adequate water supplies for the horses, mules, oxen, and travelers; and relays of teams had to be provided. Operations started September 15, 1858, the first unit from San Francisco reaching St. Louis in 23 days—the scheduled time being 25. The first coaches carried four passengers and their baggage (40 pounds free) and up to 600 pounds of mail. The team consisted of four horses or mules. The average day's drive was between 10 and 15 miles. By 1860, Butterfield's Overland Mail carried more mail than was sent by water. It continued until the Civil War closed it.

The overland route did not keep to the bottom lands of the Rio Grande Valley, but turned to the Davis Mountains because of the abundance of water there—especially in Limpia Canyon, Smith's Run, and Dead Man's Hole. This was good grass, as well as water, country; and immigrants who got an early start spent several weeks here so that their animals (which included oxen) could graze and recuperate, and so that the travelers themselves could be renewed in the cool air of the mountains.

But this road was repeatedly swept by Indian raiding parties. The Mescalero Apaches from New Mexico plundered its travelers and devastated its settlements. West of the Davis Mountains was the Comanche War Trail that crossed the San Antonio–El Paso road at Comanche Springs (now Fort Stockton). The depredations of the Comanches reached alarming proportions. So Fort Davis was established and named for Jefferson Davis, then Secretary of War.

Six companies of the Eighth U.S. Infantry occupied the site for the next seven years, spending much of their time escorting mail and freight trains, going in pursuit of raiders, and patrolling the El Paso road. A string of additional forts followed—Hudson, Lancaster, Quitman, and Stockton, to give added protection to the road. Even camels were introduced (1857–1860) to aid military patrols. But the camels did not endure because their feet were badly mutilated by the sharp rocks in ground baked into hard-pan by a searing sun.

Lieut. William H. Echols, who made his reconnaissance for water and road sites in 1860, wrote about the camels' sore feet: "Their soles have actually been abraided off to the quick by the sharp cragged rocks." He recommended that they be shoed "with a piece of circular rawhide, gathered around the leg by the slipping cord."

Peter Koch, a deep student of West Texas, thinks these camels were dromedary camels. I asked him why, and he took me south of the Davis Mountains, south indeed of Marathon, into Hell's Half Acre Ranch owned by Gage Holland. From there we traveled by jeep and came up over a razor-back ridge of sharp rocks known as the Devil's Backbone, and stopped. To the south was a single-hump mountain.

"Know its name?" he asked.

I shook my head.

"Horse Mountain," he replied.

"What has that got to do with camels?"

Peter Koch went on to explain that we were on the historic route that Echols took when he made a traverse of the country looking for water supplies. He was in desperate condition when he reached Horse Mountain at the base of which he found an abundance of water in a spring. And he wrote out in meticulous detail the story of his journey in his report to the War Department. Horse Mountain, as it is now known, was Camel's Mountain in Echols' report.

"Since there is only one hump, he must have had dromedaries with him," Peter Koch concluded.

The western outposts did not end the Indian threat; but the Civil War ended this frontier defense system in West Texas. While the Confederate Army occupied them for about a year, they were evacuated in 1862. Federal troops returned in 1867, when Fort Davis was rebuilt and occupied by the Ninth U.S. Cavalry, a newly organized colored regiment with white officers. For 15 years these troops were on escort and scouting duty, finally defeating the Apaches in 1880. That was the end of the Indian menace in West Texas; and life at Fort Davis settled pretty much into routine. The Southern Pacific constructed its line to the south of Fort Davis and the garrison rendered it some escort services. There were also occasional bandits to chase. But the Southwest was free of its major menace, and cattlemen with their great herds came to pastures of the region. Fort Davis was abandoned in 1891 and was made a National Historic Site in 1963. It was dedicated on April 4, 1966, by the First Lady, Mrs. Lyndon B. Johnson. Some 8,000 people turned out on the old parade grounds for the ceremony. Mrs. Johnson called for continued effort to preserve our heritage for the guidance of future generations. "While we continue to explore new frontiers in outer space, we must exert more effort in making the world in which we live a better and more attractive place to work, to play, and to raise our families." Texas is a good place to start, for as we shall see modern Ahabs are fast ruining the Davis Mountains.

Fort Davis was the scene of an interesting chapter in civil rights, involving Henry O. Flipper, the first Negro graduate of West Point. He was commissioned as a cavalry second lieutenant in 1877 and fought in the Indian wars of the Southwest from 1878 to 1882 when he was court-martialed and dismissed from the Army at Fort Davis. After leaving the Army, Flipper spent 37 years as a civil and mining engineer in the region, the first American Negro to gain prominence in that profession. In his memoirs, *Negro Frontiersman*, published in 1963 by Texas Western College Press, he does not give any details of the court-martial except to attribute it to prejudice against him on the part of Fort Davis' commanding officer, Col. (later Maj. Gen.) William R. Shafter.

The charges were carelessness with funds while Flipper was commissary officer. Where the truth lay, no one knows. But there are echoes of racial intolerance in the annals of the area.

At Fort Davis the Park Service has an 18-minute record of the famous old army Retreat Parade. The record was actually made at Fort Sill, Oklahoma, but it was done with the musical instruments of 1875. And the General Order which is read on this record was actually received at Fort Davis on an August afternoon of 1875, describing the military honors to be paid to former President Andrew Johnson, who had died the week before. The General Order announced to the garrison that there would be a formal parade the next morning, followed by a day of reprieve from all but the most essential duties, as a tribute to a former Commander in Chief.

The assembled buglers play "Assembly" and "Adjutant's Call," and the adjutant has the company commanders bring the units to parade rest. The band "sounds off." This consists of marching the length of the troop line and back, playing "Hail, Columbia." "Retreat" is then played, followed by the sunset gun and "To the Colors." The band then plays "The Star-Spangled Banner," a common practice in the 1870s, even though the song was not officially adopted as our national anthem until March 3, 1931 (46 Stat. 1508). The adjutant opens the ranks in the units for inspection and turns control over to the commanding officer. The band strikes up "The Young Recruit," marches to a point in front of the commanding officer, turns, moves across the parade ground, and halts facing the commanding officer. The troops then make a second circuit of the parade ground at double time while the band plays "Garryowen."

This is a fascinating record, and it makes the old parade ground come to life. Sounds that are no longer common to today's Army reach the ear—the adjutant's motions on horseback, the various sounds of cavalry, including harness noises, the jingling of sabers, and the discordant sounds of hoofbeats. With the noise of the cannon come the sound of wheels and the high-pitched, metallic rattle of the trace chain.

The cadences are slower than would be familiar either to the veterans of World War I or of World War II. The regular marching pace was 110 steps per minute and the double time 165 steps per minute, designed to maintain a close relation to the walk and trot of the cavalry.

These army Retreat parades and the formal guard mounts relieved some of the dreary routine of the fort in the 1870s and 1880s.

The machine that plays the "Retreat" over loudspeakers also sounds forth with various calls from 8 A.M. to 5 P.M. The calls are taken from the General Orders of the seventies or eighties and vary from month to month. When I was there the calls were taken from General Order No. 48, May 2, 1881, Fort Davis, Texas, and were as follows:

8:00 A.M.	Reveille
8:20	Stable Call
8:40	Breakfast
9:00	Sick Call
9:20	Fatigue Call
9:40	Assembly of Trumpeters
9:45	Assembly of Guard
10:00	Officers' Call
10:20	Watering Call
10:40	Drill Call
11:00	Officers' Call
11:20	First Sergeants' Call
11:40	Recall
12:00 Noon	Dinner
12:20 P.M.	Assembly of Trumpeters
12:40	Fatigue Call
1:00	Drill Call
1:20	Officers' Call
1:40	School Call

2:00	Recall
2:15	Attention
2:20	The General
2:40	Stable Call
3:00	Water Call
3:20	Recall, Stable
3:40	Recall, Fatigue
4:00	Fire Call
4:20	First Sergeants' Call
4:30	Assembly of Trumpeters
4:40	Assembly
4:45	Adjutants' Call
4:55	Retreat
5:00	To the Colors

These calls keep the modern Fort Davis filled with echoes of the past. One who spends a few hours in the headquarters building feels as if he is living in the environment of the old fort. I asked one secretary what she thought of this regime and laughingly she replied, "It's great. We use the 10:40 A.M. Drill Call as signal for a coffee break."

The old fort has been largely restored, as have most of the old buildings in the sense that their walls and roofs are now intact. The Commandant's home has been completely rebuilt, and other buildings have been renovated as administrative headquarters. The fort lies at the mouth of a short canyon whose walls are about 100 feet high. It was long feared that the Indians would use those cliffs to lay down a siege on the fort itself. But that never happened; the Indians saved their strength and their resources for raiding settlers' ranches and attacking wagon and mail trains. Closest to the mouth of the canyon is the old hospital. Then come the line of barracks and in front of them a spacious parade ground, with a flagpole flying a 37-star replica flag of the period. Beyond it are a stand of cottonwoods where a pure, cold spring made the place a welcome stop for any caravan.

The town of Fort Davis (5,200 feet) lies just east of the fort.

Its adobe and stucco houses flavor it with the essence of the Southwest; its cool nights, clear skies, dry, crisp air, and its closeness to cliffs, canyons, and ridges make it a welcome retreat from the desert.

McDonald Observatory, perched high on Mount Locke (6,828 feet), is also in the Davis Mountains. It was established in 1939 and is run cooperatively by the University of Texas and the University of Chicago.

In the area of Fort Davis—12 miles southwest and four miles southeast—are wind-polished rocks that have been blown into rounded shapes. The polish shows feldspar crystals, some specimens having smooth and lustrous surfaces. Some rocks are polished on all sides; others have a lee side that is less disturbed. The phenomenon is historic only, as no dunes or patches of wind-transported sand are visible. The sand, which was the abrasive, apparently was washed away by rain and stream action at times when the area knew more rainfall than it does at present. No rocks seem wind-polished higher than 12 feet above the ground and some are wind-polished only below six feet. Another theory is that these polished rocks are the work of Indians who rubbed raw hides over the surface with a mixture of sand and charcoal to remove the fat from the hides—the height of the rocks making this a plausible theory.

Mount Livermore has an oblong top that produces rough canyons on all of its sides—Madera (which means wood) on the north, Pine on the south, Goat on the west, and Limpia and Merrill on the east. It is the apex of a wild tumble of mountains.

This is rough, broken country, difficult to traverse. There are treacherous talus slopes, yawning canyons, precipitous ledges, and dangerous cliffs. Yet some ranches have used bulldozers to build jeep roads up the roughest ravines. Don McIvor heads the list, believing that it makes possible better cattle management. He told me how difficult it is for a man on horseback to find even a single cow in this wild tangle of brush and steep canyons. The road not only serves as a track for driving stock, it also attracts cattle for feeding. The reason is that they soon identify the arrival of a truck with grain or mash and at the sound of its arrival come to the road, even following the truck down the mountain in expectation of feeding.

Mule deer and the smaller white-tailed species abound in the Davis Mountains. The black bear and several species of rattlesnakes are present.

Bats are in the canyons and ring-tailed cats and raccoon, too. Skunks are numerous, and the porcupines are on the increase. Rock squirrels are common; bobcats are not uncommon; coyote and mountain lions are rare; there are gophers and a few prairie dogs; jack rabbits and cottontails are in abundance.

The Davis Mountains are of ancient origin; they are composed of igneous rock, much of it granite. Some rocks are lava; but most are crystalline, of many varieties. Occasional sandstone and limestone can be found, the latter on the northern slopes. The precipitation is about 20 inches a year and the runoffs are quick. In the skirts of the mountains a typical Chihuahua Desert vegetation is found—cacti, yuccas, sotol, and greasewood. But as one climbs, a diversity of plants is on display. This magnificent upthrust is part of the Rocky Mountain system, and one is reminded of it by the quaking aspen, limber pine, and ponderosa pine. Toward the top, Mount Livermore (sometimes called Baldy Peak) has only scrubby shrubs and scant herbs and grasses. On its north side are broken ledges where Gambel's oak, bush rock spirea, and mountain snowberry are quite common. On its southern slope are stands of gray oak (*Q. grisea*) and alligator juniper. The north side has greater vegetation due to more moisture and cooler hillsides. The granite is brightly painted with lichens— orange, red, yellow, and gray.

High, shaded areas have meadow rue, Arizona sage, wild geranium, and bedstraw, and high open spots, prickly pear and the golden aster. My pilgrimage to Mount Livermore was in January, when the high country was far from its best. At this elevation flowers and grasses head up after mid-August and the prime time of flowering is the month of September.

In some canyons quaking aspen and Gambel's oak grow in mixed, thick stands. Gooseberries, Virginia creeper, ferns, and elderberry persist on talus slopes.

The lower reaches up to 6,000 feet show a wood combination common over much of the Southwest—the gray oak, piñon pine, and alligator juniper. When the alligator juniper is thick, it casts a bluish, silver sheen over a slope or a valley. The century plant (from which an intoxicating liquor is made) and mountain mahogany (that makes a hot, slow-burning fire) are found in this oak-pine-juniper area.

Overgrazing, which is characteristic of the Davis Mountains, causes the piñon pine and juniper to come in. I saw their extensive encroachment at the higher elevations. The ranchers try to exterminate them, the Federal government paying half the cost. Yet not much of this work is done. Don McIvor, conservation-minded owner of the U Up and U Down Ranch, does some clearing. But he is mostly content to let the porcupines, greatly on the increase, do the thinning. The day I went to Livermore with him we saw dozens upon dozens of trees girdled by the porcupine who loves especially the inner cambium layer of the bark of pine trees.

The ponderosa pine is found in open canyons above 6,000 feet and grows in thick stands 80 feet or more high. And mistletoe commonly infests it. Chokecherries decorate this zone.

Above 7,000 feet is limber pine. It was that tree, not the ponderosa, which was much sought after last century, especially for sills and doors, as it is pitchy and its lumber preserves well. Fort Davis had logging camps around Livermore. The sites of its former camps are easily found and its old logging roads easy to follow. Those army crews took out all the huge limber pine in the area and not enough time has passed in the intervening century to produce trees of like girth. But younger ones are on their way.

The old army logging sites are fertile spots for artifacts—square nails, bolts, cartridges, mule shoes, and arrowheads.

More recent relics, dating into this century, are woodcutters' huts made of small juniper logs. For many years the U Up and U Down had crews working high up, in family groups, cutting and piling wood in cords. U Up and U Down sold this wood for fuel in the Alpine, Marathon, Marfa areas before oil burners came in.

As I traveled up Madera Canyon to Livermore, I saw flocks of 30 to 40 band-tailed pigeons who had congregated in treetops near pens where cattle were fed grain. There were also signs of wild turkey, though I saw none. They were imported in the 1920s and according to Don McIvor are "barely holding their own." Predators are numerous and they take their toll. And the dry, windy weather which accompanied the drought of the fifties and early sixties was also hard on the turkey population. High up with the turkeys are quail, jays, and canyon wrens.

North of Livermore are walnut trees—more than a foot thick and more than 50 feet high. Under secluded low bluffs are Emory's oak, Texas red oak, Mexican mulberry, and hackberry. In the larger canyons, where water is more common, the maple and red haw are found and with them wild cherry and Arizona grape willow. Ash appear along watercourses; and occasional madrone (*Arbutus texana*) shows up, plum bushes can be found, the silver-leaf oak (*Q. hypolencoides*), whose white underleaves are conspicuous in a breeze, is common, and at least 14 ferns are present.

Relic forests are part of the priceless heritage of the area. Walnuts, ponderosa pine, limber pine, aspen, maple, red haw, cherries—these all belong to other climes. But they once flourished here when the rainfall was heavy and the humidity high—in the Pleistocene—a million years or more ago. Like the relic forests of the Chisos, those of the Davis Mountains show how sturdy and persevering nature can be.

Some of the flowers, too, are throwbacks to times when there was greater rainfall and more humidity. The spurges, scorpion weed, chickweed, wormwood, pigweed, and sage are identified in our minds with the desert. So is the buckthorn from which cascara is obtained and which is plentiful in the Davis Mountains—and the tobacco plant, beard grass, and cocklebur. But these mountains also have vetch and wild roses reminiscent of more northern climes. Here is yarrow as plain and homely as any in the Sierra Nevada. The catchfly that I know at my home in Goose Prairie, Washington, is present. The lichen, known in northern

Minnesota as "tripe of the rock," is here. The fleabane, gentian, ragwort, and penstemon of the Rockies are common.

The little poison ivy is occasionally found. The shamrock-shaped oxalis looks as if it's been transported from Maine. The columbine of Oregon's Wallowas is present. Honeysuckle, as pretty and as pestiferous as any in the Potomac Valley, grows here. The harebell which I find in my own Cascades in Washington flourishes high in these mountains. And the flax—the exact species Lewis and Clark discovered in Idaho—is quite at home in the Davis Mountains.

There has never been much federally owned land in Texas. The Joint Resolution of the Congress for the annexation of Texas to the Union declared that Texas was to retain all vacant and unappropriated lands within its borders to be applied to the payment of its debts and the balance to be disposed of as Texas directed. The United States was ceded only barracks, posts, harbors, magazines, docks, navy yards, and the like pertaining to the public defense and belonging to the Republic.

Great areas were opened by the state to veterans and to pioneer residents; the railroad received generous grants; immense areas were sold and settlement by ranchers was encouraged; the university and the "free-school fund" received large grants. But very little to date has gone into state parks and the like. While Texas owns some land and is authorized to purchase it for state purposes or to condemn it, no state program of any size for setting aside wilderness areas for recreation has been launched. Texas has not done at the state level what the Federal government has done with its public lands in the realm of conservation.

When it comes to state parks and state forests, Texas is far, far behind the other states. She has no program that can compare with New York's, California's, North Carolina's, or Minnesota's. And even those latter states, which are deemed progressive when it comes to outdoor recreational programs, are far behind the need measured by the expanding population. In other words, Texas, when it comes to outdoor recreation facilities, is as underdeveloped as the benighted nations of Asia, Africa, and Latin America are when it comes to a modern agricultural and industrial system.

We stood on the saddle between Madera and Limpia canyons, right under Livermore. Don McIvor and his wife were there; so were Jim Bowmer, Peter Koch, and Dr. Barton Warnock, the distinguished botanist and biologist of Sul Ross College. We were mostly silent as we ate Mrs. McIvor's delicious lunch, for we were all overwhelmed with the beauty of the scene.

The Sierra del Carmen Range of Mexico had a purplish cast on the far horizon.

A huge piñon pine, two or three feet in diameter, stands at the saddle.

Two golden eagles soared overhead.

"They are now nesting," Peter Koch said. "This is January and their young hatch out in March."

With glasses we closely inspected the trees at the base of the ledge that tops Livermore. The quaking aspen were unmistakable. One large conifer gave rise to discussion.

"It's a Douglas fir," McIvor said.

"There are none in the Davis Mountains," Dr. Warnock answered.

"Only the one," was the reply.

But the issue could not be resolved, as a lowering sun prevented us from making the traverse to the point and returning to the low country before dark.

We talked of the legends of this country. One is that a famous Indian chief had been buried on top of Livermore and that his remains, when discovered, had been carefully transported to the Smithsonian Institution in Washington, D.C. The discovery went back, it is said, to 1895. Peter Koch explained how legend sometimes grows from quite different facts. It seems that the Indians had hidden arrow points in a crevice on the highest point of Livermore. They were sun worshipers—the Sun being the Father and the Earth their Mother. The arrowheads were cached at a point which would be the first to receive the morning light and the last to be touched by the setting sun. They were, in other words, deposited there as solemn ceremonials and are now in the possession of the West Texas Historical and Scientific Society. But no person was ever buried there. As they told me later at the Smithsonian, "No skeletons are here from any place in Jeff Davis County."

On Livermore, we also talked at length about the future of the country. With the exception of McIvor's, Eppenauer's, and Kokernot's holdings it is greatly overgrazed. Perhaps in time it will be so mutilated that the owners will want the state or Federal government to bail them out. That may someday create a sentiment for the creation of a park. But there is no such sentiment at present; and the trend seems toward a different kind of public participation.

The Davis Mountain ranchers, like others, lease hunting rights to outsiders. McIvor has about 70 deer hunters a season and has provided a special building to house them at his upper ranch that lies at 6,000 feet. Other ranchers follow suit. And there is growing interest in the Food and Agriculture Act of 1962 (76 Stat. 605) and the Regulation (C. F. R. Title 6, Pt. 321) under §401 of that Act by which the Farmers Home Administration gives ranchers Federal financial assistance for providing recreational facilities to members of the public.

The Davis Mountains are an exciting segment of our wilderness facilities. They are rich in history, rich in life and beauty. They are mainly in private ownership. Yet many of our national shrines are privately or locally owned. Mount St. Helens in my state of Washington is owned by a private company. Some lakes in the High Sierra are owned by municipalities hundreds of miles distant. Giant redwoods in California are privately owned. Whoever may be the owner in law, shrines such as these and the Great Stone Face in New Hampshire belong in a sense to everyone in the country.

Their beauty is the inheritance of all the people. If they are overgrazed or denuded of trees, water tables the region over are destroyed and floods take place many miles distant. What ranchers do to the Davis Mountains to make another dollar often affects the welfare and happiness of faraway people. The very existence of the Davis Mountains in West Texas is a thrill to a New Englander or to one who comes from the Pacific West. To have a high mountain mass in a desert environment for exploration is a real treat—what I like to think of as a dividend of national citizenship. The Davis Mountains rising high out of the Chihuahua Desert are indeed a shrine. With our burgeoning population they will become more and more precious with the passing years.

Texas must be educated to recognize these shrines and to protect them. Ruthless private enterprise and a callous disregard of the public interest have not yet ruined the Davis Mountains; but they have come close to it. And if they have their way the Davis Mountains will go the way of the Big Thicket, far to the east.

CHAPTER VII

CAPOTE FALLS

Capote Falls is a blue-bright falls in a desert. Its cold, fresh water comes off a 200-foot cliff in the bleak, barren Sierra Viejo Mountains of Texas, forming a small creek a few yards wide and perhaps a dozen miles long. When storms come in the summer, the little stream becomes a torrent that pours its angry waters down a barren arroyo to the Rio Grande. For most of the year it is a clear thread of water that can be jumped at almost any point until it finally is lost in the desert.

To reach Capote Falls one goes west of the Big Bend National Park on Route 170, known as the River Road or Camino del Rio. This hard-surfaced road is one of our most picturesque, vying for beauty with the Columbia Gorge in Oregon and Washington. Most of the time it is at water level and is indeed in the gorge of the Rio Grande much of the way. But there are stretches where it climbs to a height, and one who parks his car can hike to a nearby pinnacle for an even grander view. The walls of the gorge are mainly basalt, like those of the Columbia Gorge. But while the latter show layer on layer of lava flows, the Rio Grande shows a wild array of huge rocks that have tumbled from the heights where a lava intrusion once boiled from the earth, slowly to crumble and crack. There are no trees except an occasional

mesquite. Yucca, ocotillo, sotol, and many cacti grow in profusion. The picture is mostly one of emptiness and desolation.
Yet the brown stream of the river marks greenness and life. Every
available flat has been watered. Cotton and vegetables are grown.
Most prized of all are the melons—the Presidio melons that are
perhaps as sweet as those grown along the drier sections of the
Columbia in Oregon. The green strip following the meandering
river is brightened by cottonwood trees. Some keep their tinted
leaves through the winter, not to lose them until fresh buddings
come in February. These stately trees in the narrow green belts
that follow the river are restful to the eyes. The skies of this part
of Texas are unusually bright and the reflections from the rocky,
barren wastes are fierce. The cottonwoods and melon patches
become hallowed oases in a desert.

North and east of Presidio is the old silver-mining town of
Shafter. Cottonwoods shade this sunburned ghost town where
4,000 people once lived on both sides of Cibolo Creek now crossed
by a suspension bridge. Today there are only roofless houses with
staring windows and crumbling stone and adobe walls. Mesquite
trees and prickly-pear cactus grow out of the rubble. A barren
cemetery holding about 2,000 bodies is marked by stones and by
metal and wooden crosses and by a few plastic flowers.

The Chaniti Mountains to the west are usually draped in blue
velvet shadows, but the wind that blows off them is hot. Here
silver was discovered in 1882 and worked until 1942; a brief
attempt to reactivate the mines in 1952 ended in failure. Shafter
died as a result of several forces: the low price of silver, an
ore that became poorer, labor troubles, and water problems in
the deep, winding tunnels which extend 150 miles underground.
These tunnels became flooded and no pumps could be found to
cope with them. I walked the deserted streets of this old ghost
town and crossed the Cibolo, where watercress flourishes, by the
footbridge. On the far side were a few adobe houses occupied

by Americans of Mexican ancestry. Children in scant, ragged clothes cried shrilly as they played ball. Two men carried in a huge mesquite tree for a fireplace where beans were to be baked and tortillas made.

This countryside, apart from the river bottoms, is seared and brown most of the year. Even in winter, however, it acquires a light green nap following a heavy rain. And in the spring, when the cactus is in bloom, when the wildflowers come, when tender shoots of grasses appear, a fresh green mantle extends to the horizon. The spring flowering comes early. Even in February the bluebonnets of Texas are appearing. This member of the lupine family has several species. The showiest, the largest, the most spectacular is *Lupinus navardii* of the Big Bend Country; but by legislative enactment back in 1901 *Lupinus subcarnosus* became the official flower of Texas. It is restricted largely to southern Texas. Few, however, know this; and the dainty bluebonnets that begin to show before winter is over are greeted with the same affection as though they were the official species. And the "Bluebonnet Song," which is now the "Texas State Flower Song," sings of all bluebonnets, not only the restricted *Lupinus subcarnosus.*

The hard-surfaced road now ends at Presidio, a border town whose counterpart in Mexico is Ojinaga. They are connected by a rickety bridge. Americans in search of good food usually cross over to dine in a Mexican restaurant. The people of Ojinaga do practically all of their shopping in Presidio.

Alvar Nunez Cabeza DeVaca, who visited Presidio in 1534, saw a settlement of adobe dwellings with nearby cultivated strips. So Presidio is probably our oldest continuously inhabited town. At least that is what they say in Presidio. This border town has been under six flags—Spain, 1519; France, 1685; Spain, 1690; Mexico, 1821; Texas, 1836; United States, 1845; Southern Confederacy, 1861; United States, 1865.

The town of Presidio is unincorporated, which means that there are few municipal services. Its inhabitants, like members of a village, are pretty much on their own when it comes to water supply, sewage, fire protection, and so on. The streets are unpaved; a gravel runway serves as an airport; hotel and motel facilities are scarce. One-storied shops line the main street. Daytime winter temperatures are in the seventies and at night drop as low as 15° F. Summer temperatures soar. I asked Dick L. Cross of the Philip's Motel about the severity of summer heat. He became downright indignant. "The only reason Presidio has the reputation of being hot is the Weather Bureau has an observer here. It's not nearly as hot as Needles, California, or Yuma, Arizona." And he added, "Our mean annual temperature is $\frac{1}{2}$ a degree higher than Houston, Texas." Yet 117° F. is hot, Weather Bureau or not. But the nights are cool, as the humidity is low at this elevation of 2,400 feet. In the winter the fog often hangs low over the river, as the warm rocks of the basin condense the cold, moist air that often moves in with a "norther" and produces a mantle thicker than the dust that sometimes envelops the Rio Grande.

The road west of Presidio is gravel and runs not much beyond Candelaria, the last substantial village on the Rio Grande east of El Paso. This is a road so treacherous in stretches that, come a Texas norther and a heavy rain, automobiles mire and have to be "tailed out," as they say when a critter gets stuck in a mudhole.

In the winter the river at Presidio has two to three feet of water, for the town lies below the point where the Rio Conchos comes roaring in from Mexico. But 40 miles upstream, at Candelaria, the Rio Grande is dry. There is not a bucket of water in the arroyo most of the year. When there are storms and heavy rains—as in July—the river will run at Candelaria. But those days are not many. The dry arroyo is an easy passageway to and from Mexico; and it is a boon to the people of San Antonio—the Mexican counterpart of Candelaria—as they do their shopping in this country.

When Candelaria was settled near the turn of the century, the river was full. A U.S. Army post was there; and settlers were wanted to grow wheat for local consumption. Wheat was grown. But today only cotton, not even the sweet Presidio melon, is raised. The reason is the water.

The Rio Grande runs through thirsty country, its water being in great demand. The Federal government built two dams north of El Paso—Elephant Butte (1915) and Caballo (1938); and they left no water for Candelaria. Elephant Butte was conceived in the 1890s as a private undertaking. But the courts enjoined it because its impoundment of the waters of the Rio Grande would adversely affect the navigability of the lower reaches of the river. The Congress, which has exclusive control over navigable streams, can, however, destroy navigability. As a result of Elephant Butte and Caballo, there is no river water for irrigation at Candelaria. Drilled wells are used; but well water at Candelaria, like that at Presidio, is slightly salty, and the only crop that seems to prosper is cotton.

The U.S. Army post is no more and Candelaria has now shrunk to 13 families, except during the fall and winter when Mexican migrants come in to pick and chop cotton, raising the total to some 47 families.

The first settler was J. J. Kilpatrick. His granddaughters, Frances Howard and Mrs. J. E. Walker, run the old cotton gin and the general store that he built, and the filling station as well. They are a wholesome influence in the town, keeping it spick-and-span. Tamarisk trees, two stately cypresses, and two arbor vitae adorn their place.

Five of us stopped there for a lunch of cheese, crackers, and cold drinks and as we left were asked to sign the visitors' book. A couple of months later we returned, without Jim Bowmer, and once more had lunch there. This time the ladies said they had noticed, after we had left, that one of us was a Justice of the Supreme Court.

"Which one was it?" asked Bob Burleson.

"The one who isn't here this time," was the reply. And that is how Bowmer became known as Justice Jim.

This dry, wind-blown land has no lawns—no green ground cover except cotton. Cotton covers the broad valley that lies on both sides of the boundary, giving Candelaria the pleasant aspect of an oasis. It is marked on the Mexican side by an isolated rock wall emerging from the earth and standing distant from the mountains in the background. It is called *pilon,* meaning boundary-marker stone.

A Catholic church, well maintained, whitewashed and adorned by a few elms, stands on a hillside overlooking the village; and nearby is the public school. Between the church and the school is the city jail. It stands in isolation on the same hillside. It has, according to one villager, "the best view in all of West Texas." It is unique in another respect, as it is not a building but a cage— roughly a six-foot cube. I have never seen it occupied but it is praised throughout the region. It serves the ancient function of the stock in New England history. And as one person put it, "A wife has no trouble locating her husband."

The general store offers a wide variety of products from clothing to groceries and carries the best cheese I have known. Near the entrance is a myna bird that speaks only Spanish. *"Tiene usted piojos?"* which literally translated means "Have you any lice?"

Candelaria is a devout Catholic village and when the Christmas season comes, it witnesses moving rites. For nine nights before Christmas the youngsters, organized into choral groups, go from house to house carrying miniature images of the Christ Child, Mary, and the manger, and performing what is known as the Posados. Half of the group enters a home while the other half stays outside for a serenade. The outside group sings, asking for admission. The inside group responds, saying there is no room in the house. The request and the response go on, over and again, hour after hour. Finally the interior group relents and lets the Christ Child in; and the relics representing Him, Mary, and the manger are left in that house until the next night when the same ceremony is performed before another home.

May third is the day of Santa Cruz (the discovery of the Holy Cross). The prior night bonfires are lit on the hills. The people gather, carrying a cross and placing it on a hill as they sing and pray.

May 15 is the day of San Ysidro, the saint of the fields. The families assemble when the head of the village fires a pistol. They carry a box that contains the figure or picture of San Ysidro. They march from field to field, praying for rain, and leave the box under a tree. When the rain starts, they remove the box and give thanks.

Perhaps I have lingered too long in Shafter, Presidio, and Candelaria. But any traveler to Capote Falls should do the same. An oasis in a bleak, barren land is always welcome. And Capote Falls is memorable not only for its beauty but also for the environment in which it flows.

Capote Falls is some 16 miles from Candelaria, and the dirt road that crosses empty, rolling land is unmarked. A gravel landing strip for small planes appears. A power line—built by REA—comes out of nowhere, headed for remote ranches in the Sierra Viejo Mountains, dominated by Candelaria Peak (6,560 feet). In a few miles somber, barren gullies are replaced by a Painted Desert. The words are not on any map; they are my own. But to my eyes this desert is as bright and brilliant and as unique as any of our better-known displays, including Bryce Canyon.

This part of Texas has primarily sedimentary rocks on display. They are deposits made when the area was under water. Wind, frost, and water have been eroding them for thousands of

years; and they now appear to be islands or isolated buttes or solitary mesas in a broad plain. To the north are the Sierra Viejo Mountains, whose rim, known as Candelaria Rim, is of lava. But the intermediate hills are sandstone and limestone and some of them volcanic tuff. There are pinks and whites, yellows and brown. The shades vary with the position of the sun, the gayest colors being shown by a lowering sun. A layer of pink may be overlaid with a layer of white. A distant bluish tinge has a foreground of green. The paints have been wildly distributed without rhyme or reason. There is no pattern to the design, only infinite variety. Yet each alcove is a place of rare beauty.

The volcanic tuff has hardened and been sculptured by weather into Corinthian columns, into concave surfaces, into tall, spindly columns, into an infinite variety of designs; and in a lowering sun the hard-packed, polished tuff often shines like marble.

What I enjoy the most are the pinkish areas overlaid by loose blackish lava rock from the size of eggs to the size of basketballs. The earth on which they rest has obviously been washed and swept over and again, each operation making the loose rocks only more vivid. The erosion under them has indeed been so great that some seem to be perched and recently arrived.

These loose lava rocks are travelers from distant areas. Some believe they were blown here from California or the Rockies. I like to think that is true, for I can visualize nothing more theatrical than the Painted Desert during a hailstorm of lava rock.

In the winter one can walk a hundred yards in this bright land without finding a blade of grass. Only greasewood, ocotillo, and cactus seem to grow. But there are fences with gates to open, for up ahead somewhere in the faraway hills are cattle. The entrance to Capote Canyon is marked by a gate and once cleared only a mile or so remains to the start of the trail. An aluminum barn gives the impression of habitation that is illusory. No one lives here. Stone walls of former structures still stand. They mark the site of a hostel serving the schooners or stagecoaches drawn by horses that crossed a pass on Candelaria Mountain to Marfa. The old dirt road with its many switchbacks is still visible as it works its way over the mountain, though rock-slides have made it impassable even to jeeps. At this hostel, horses were changed or added for the long pull out of the valley. Through this passage moved all the cotton of Candelaria on its way to market. Also the Capote Canyon once was mined for nitrate.

The operators put a 250-horsepower Carliss steam engine here with a boiler, evaporators, redwood tanks, and a ball mill with hooper, conveyors, and pumps. This was the equipment for proc-essing nitrate extracted from the bottom of the rim rock in a sub-limated layer under the basalt. The experts say that a tremendous deposit is there. The plant went into operation November 11, 1918, but not a penny was ever realized. What was mined was taken to market by horse-drawn schooners that brought in on return trips all the supplies for Capote Falls, Candelaria, and the other river settlements.

The entrance to Capote Canyon is marked by the ruins of an old adobe hut, dominated by an ancient cottonwood. The immediate scene is dreary. But the site itself is one of the most dramatic for a residence that I know. As one looks west, the Sierra Viejo Mountains mark an intimate barrier on the north. As far as the eye can see to the south and west are buttes, mesas, broken escarpments, and rolling plains. No living thing appears except a raven high overhead. The solitude has depth and color, too. The dazzling brightness of an overhead sun disappears by midafternoon and the purples reappear in distant hills. There are shades of pink and green and gray in the shafts of light through a cloudy sky. This is wonderland without end, every hour painting a new and different scene. Someday there should be a hostel here—the headquarters for the glories that lie up Capote Canyon to the east.

It is not much more than two miles to the falls. The trail crosses and recrosses the creek many times—water that contains so much nitrate that if one cuts himself and washes in it, a scab develops in about ten minutes. Cottonwood trees are scattered sparingly along the waterway. More numerous is the Arizona ash, which grows mostly in the stream bed. On the embankments high above the stream are mesquite; and one who hikes there can see why Texas ranchers boasted that they often "dug" for their wood. The roots of the mesquite are as large as the trunk. They extend great distances underground as this thirsty tree searches for water. The whole story is plain for the beginner to see as he walks to Capote Falls.

There are scatterings of willow as well as ash along the watercourse; and about a half-mile up a narrow canyon makes off to the south and leads in a few hundred yards to a hot springs, which has no detectable medicinal quality. But the water is hot and ample enough for bathing; and it forms a modest tributary to Capote.

The tracks of mule deer multiply as the visitor nears the head of the canyon; and if he has patience he can usually see some high on the rocks. Evidence of their presence is so plentiful that my impression is that mule deer far outnumber cattle in the Capote area.

Capote Creek had recently been in flood, for there were wet patches and small pools of water several feet higher than the normal winter flow. But the water at this stage is always clear and cold. It is a soft water good to drink; and it is cold enough to maintain trout should they be planted.

The rim of the winding canyon above the creek is composed of basalt and there are places where it has streaks of white. The weather was so cold when I first saw it and we were so close on the heels of a "norther" that I thought it was snow. But Peter Koch put me right—the white was guano from roosts of vultures.

Near the head of the canyon are stands of basket grass, the species used by the Indians for making baskets. The ash grow larger and thicker; huge basalt rocks must be climbed; and then, as one rounds a rocky turn, Capote Falls appears in an amphitheater hemmed in on three sides by towering cliffs. Huge ash trees cover a spit of sand with their branches; and it is here one sits for hours watching the quiet beauty of the scene.

Capote Falls is in three sections—the first drop of six or eight feet is in the form of cascades; the next 30 feet are a funnel of water falling to a ledge; the last 100 feet are thin braids of water falling over rock. The rock is mostly igneous though there is some limestone. The water carries minerals in saturation, and transpiration is so great that minute particles of the minerals are deposited as the water falls. The result is the formation of a stalagmite—not in a cone but as a mantle over which the water pours. The mantle is indeed in the form of the cape used by bullfighters—*capote* in Spanish. This capote becomes realistic indeed when sunlight drenches it, for it gives off a yellowish tinge.

The overhang of the cliff is marked by the cementlike nests of the rough-winged swallow. The falls which are not in full sunlight until May are adorned at the base by thick beds of columbine and maidenhair fern. The bloom of the columbine brings a blaze of yellow to the falls.

The columbine (*Aquilegia*) is Hinckley's species and in Texas is found only in this canyon. A scraggly shrub about four feet high with branches almost leafless and known as Mormon tea is here. Its name is *Ephedra* and its male plants show yellow clusters in springtime. The cockroach plant (*Halophyton*), rarely found in Texas, is also here. The plant is ground and mixed with corn meal and used as a poison for cockroaches. A wild mustard (*Lesquerella*) whose seeds give forth a fine machine oil is present.

Capote Canyon is rarely wider than 100 yards and usually narrower; and at the falls huge rockslides from the north and west have made it even smaller. A dozen people at the falls is a crowd—so small is the space. Moreover, the creek-bed channel and the path along it are so narrow that they can accommodate but a few people at a time. The result is that this is a fragile wilderness that would be quickly ruined by the multitudes.

If Capote Falls is to be preserved as a park or a monument, as it must be, it needs special safeguards. This is not a place for unescorted tourists. The crowds would soon trample it to dust. The precincts of Capote Falls should be invaded only by guided tours. That would provide some protection to the Canyon and it would help the outsider understand that this is a place for worship, not for a frolic. The beauty is so fragile, the solitude is so precious that the Canyon is only for those who walk reverently.

The life of Capote Falls is in the *ciénega* on the limestone escarpment high above them. This escarpment, which runs for some miles, overlooks the valley of the Rio Grande and is more than matched by the parallel massive escarpment in Mexico. The chasm in between is mostly parched land, now that the river has no water between El Paso and Presidio. The slopes and side canyons abound in deer. The escarpment is marked not only by Capote Falls, but by Split Rock, a few miles north, where a Marfa group has established a relay tower to pick up TV broadcasts from El Paso.

Hiking the escarpment is an exhilarating experience. The abyss at one's feet seems bottomless. The distant purples add mystery and magic. The wind whines out of the void; even the vibration of the scattered bunch grass is audible. There is solitude and desolation; beauty and emptiness. On this escarpment it always seems that I am the only living thing, possessed of all the earthly expanse that stretches to infinity.

The 15 sections around the *ciénega* were the original unit

acquired by Lucas C. Brite in 1885, a young man who "didn't chew tobacco or whittle," as one old-timer put it.

A New Yorker, John Drohan, first owned this *ciénega* land. He sold it to Robert A. Nixon, an Englishman, who in turn sold out to Brite, whose brand was a Bar Cross:

$$\overline{+}$$

Brite was one of many who came out of East Texas, driving 140 Longhorn cattle 600 miles and looking for new grasslands. By 1880 the grasslands east of the Pecos were pretty well taken up and the westward movement of cattle was under way. This Big Bend country was practically unknown to cattlemen—apart from its reputation of being hard, bitter land without grass or water. But Eastern cattle prices were high—$40 a head—while in West Texas the animals sold for $3 or $4. The lure of riches beckoned cattlemen on; and the prospect of using the branding iron to make another man's cattle one's own brought on the adventurers. By the mid-eighties, when the Southern Pacific reached Marathon, Alpine, and Marfa, long, dusty lines of cattle came by the thousands to these dry lands. When Luke Brite drove his herd to Capote and settled there, the grama grass was so high that the horses pulling the covered wagon could nip it as they walked in harness.

Today the Highland Hereford claims West Texas. Originally it was the Longhorn that was long of wind, leg, and horn, as the cattlemen say, and ideal for this country. Distances were long between water holes and the Longhorn was good at traveling. As J. Frank Dobie says in *The Longhorns*, the animal in time of drought, when the grass disappeared, lived like a deer on cactus and brush. It consumed the huge bloom stalks of the Spanish dagger and got the water it needed from the prickly pear. Its mouth was as tough as a goat's; its hardihood in the desert was equaled only by the burro. It was free-running and pretty well took care of itself on the open range, not requiring the care and attention needed by the Hereford. But it could not compete on the market. As Gage Holland of Marathon told me, "The Longhorn is like the buffalo—all its meat is up front and the public wants the steaks that come from the rear end."

Today a few ranchers raise Longhorns as a hobby, merely to keep the species alive. None is raised commercially. When the conversion to Herefords took place, some Longhorns still frequented remote gullies and escarpments and became wild. Virginia Madison, in *The Big Bend Country*, relates how these

wild ones stampeded Hereford herds and became a nuisance, causing ranchers to hunt them down and kill them.

Luke Brite kept watch over his Longhorns (which he began to replace with Herefords in 1896) from a home he built in a limestone cave. His place was barren and primitive. As the settlers increased, he went into business selling Arbuckle coffee and used the wooden crates in which it came to build walls outside the cave against weather.

In the early days of West Texas the earliest type of building was the dugout—a room below the ground covered with logs and soil and often walled with stone. These dugouts were cool in summer and warm in winter. Log houses were out of the question as there were no cedar or oak logs—indeed no trees except in the upper reaches of the Chisos and Davis Mountains and along the Rio Grande. So Luke Brite, living underground, was living in good West Texas style.

A schoolteacher, Miss Eddie Anderson, came to a nearby ranch as a teacher for the children; and soon she and Luke were married. Then they built the old one-storied adobe hut that still stands near the *ciénega*.

Cattle ranchers found it hard sledding, even with the railroad supplying access to the Eastern markets. Luke Brite's neighbors gradually gave up, and Luke bought them out. He would get their land at a price and take over their cattle on consignment. His sellers were always in distress, so he acquired tract after tract cheap. Buying in this way at the bottom, he built a solid cattle empire. Overgrazing was a constant scourge, and it increased the severity of the plague of the drought. So he went in for dry farming on some of his lands. Several miles east of the escarpment are the Flats, a broad expanse of rolling land. Here he planted hay and erected silos to hold it.

Brite also established a store at his Headquarters Ranch, opening it to the public and competing price-wise with merchants located on the faroff railway at Marfa. Brite, Texas, became a post office, too; and the Headquarters Ranch was something of a community center.

We traversed this area before coming to the ranch house, pitted with bullet holes from Pancho Villa's guerrillas. They raided this border in 1916 and 1917. On Christmas Day, 1917, forty mounted bandits surrounded the Brite ranch house after first cutting the telephone wires. The Brites barricaded the house and opened fire. An intermediary was sent by the Mexicans demanding surrender. The Brites refused, but knowing they were outnumbered, surrendered the keys to a store that was heavily stocked with provisions. The bandits rounded up Brite's horses and saddled them for riding, using their own animals for packing out clothes, flour, canned goods, and other provisions from the storehouse.

During the raid, Mickey Welch, who carried the mail from Valentine to Candelaria, arrived with two Mexican passengers. Welch was hanged and the two passengers shot. Guests of the Brites, the Reverend Mr. H. M. Bandy and family, arrived for Christmas dinner; and the guerrillas, learning that he was a padre, let him through the lines. Word of the conflict reached Marfa through some neighbors; and the U.S. cavalrymen came over from Fort D. A. Russell at Marfa—all in Model-T Fords, led by a colonel in a Dodge. They pressed the pursuit closely until the bandits came to the escarpment where the automobiles had to stop, the bandits disappearing down the escarpment across the valley toward Mexico, while the soldiers, without any horses, plodded on foot. Later horses were obtained and the pursuit renewed, 18 guerrillas being killed including the leader, Pinto Villa Nueva.

The present foreman, Wells, who had just arrived at the Brite ranch, told me that the loot of the bandits was scattered over the 10 miles between the ranch house and Capote Falls, near which they descended from the escarpment.

The Brite ranch is distant and remote, its buildings swallowed up by an intense solitude. It is a place where a traveler is always welcome, even a lonely "wet back" on his way out of Mexico looking for a job. When we reached the ranch Mr. Wells said, even though we came by car, "It's getting kind of late, so you-all better tie up for the night."

The Brite ranch flourished until the 1950s. Dr. William E. Vandevere of El Paso told me that he visited the *ciénega* in 1947 and that it was then an ideal marsh lined with Bermuda grasses and marked by cattails and sedges. The water oozed out from a thousand seepage points. Water and flora were one biotic community, living in harmony and producing a steady flow for Capote Falls.

The waters of the *ciénega* were so plentiful that a lake was formed by a dam and the water used by the cattle, by the occupants of the Headquarters Ranch, and by ministers for out-of-doors baptismal services. For years the place was rich in game including wild turkeys, ducks, and geese. And Capote Falls ran many times the volume it runs today. Jim White, who runs the Brite ranch, told me that this country will sustain no more than three cattle to a section. That safeguard was honored for years. But finally disaster struck.

In the 1950s a severe drought settled on the land. In desperation some foreman put 1,800 head of Hereford into the *ciénega* where only 45 should have been. They stayed for two months, and I saw the devastation they caused. The Bermuda grass has gone. So have the cattails and most of the sedges. There are patches of marshes left but mostly deep-gutted gullies. Mesquite —whose presence speaks eloquently of erosion—has arrived in thick, vigorous stands. It's a thirsty plant that will suck the place dry. Water no longer seeps slowly, but runs fast. Flash floods could now ruin the *ciénega*.

A waterfall in the desert is a miracle. Man's act in destroying it is depredation. Capote Falls must have a protective arm around it—either state or Federal. The free enterprise of the cattle business is too capricious, too irresponsible to be entrusted with the preservation of this, a great wonder of America.

The hard-surfaced road—River Road or Camino del Rio—that now ends at Presidio will soon be extended to Candelaria and on west, so that thousands of tourists will roar by the front door of Capote Falls. The falls will soon not be remote and distant, but as accessible as hundreds of our other natural wonders. The new hard-surfaced road will plainly put Capote Falls into the public domain. It should become an urgent Federal project. Some two miles of the creek must be included and the falls themselves. In addition, some of the old Brite ranch must be added so that the *ciénega* can be protected and forever guarded against invasion by livestock. The total acreage needed would be well over the minimum we have set for wilderness areas. The size of the project qualifies it for federal promotion. The combination of the Painted Desert, the creek, the falls, the *ciénega,* the escarpment, and the rolling top country will make it one of the most powerful magnets in all the Southwest.

This Federal project is a *must,* for Texas says it has no funds for that purpose. There are hundreds of millions of dollars in Texas for the promotion of right-wing political and educational programs, but not many dollars for private ventures to save pieces of our outdoor heritage. Nature Conservancy in New York, privately financed, has saved many tracts from destruction, as I have related in A *Wilderness Bill of Rights.* It has taken over where Federal interest and state concern are absent. A combination of Nature Conservancy and state park activities has worked wonders in Pennsylvania. But Texas, still fighting the battle of socialism of the last century (a park is socialism, isn't it?), has not yet entered the present century when it comes to preserving large areas of its wonderland for outdoor recreation.

CHAPTER VIII

THE GOLDEN EAGLE

The golden eagle (*Aquila chrysaetos canadensis*) is monarch of the mountains. The light gold on the neck is a field mark. But when the bird wheels, it shows the upper surface, the white tail, with its dark terminal band, and that is the sure method of identifying it. The ranchers of West Texas swear they can identify the golden eagle in any posture or position. And they also swear at it.

Ranchers say the golden eagles take their calves. They told me that golden eagles kill 85 per cent to 90 per cent of all antelope fawns, that they kill from 50 per cent to 60 per cent of the lambs of sheep and goats. "Any animal that kills our property is the enemy. Right?" asked one irate rancher in the Valentine area. "Then we should kill it."

"That man's as sullen as a mule in a mudhole," Justice Jim Bowmer observed.

"I'd say different," Peter Koch added. "He's mean enough to suck eggs and cunning enough to hide the shells."

Golden eagle eat carrion especially in cold weather and they will be seen eating the carcasses of dead animals including the jack rabbits killed by automobiles on the highways of West Texas. But the fact that they are carrion eaters is not conclusive proof

156

that they kill what they eat. It is, however, conclusive to West Texas ranchers who inveigh against the golden eagle and its advocate, the Audubon Society.

The golden eagle, on the average, eats 10 ounces of meat a day, which adds up to 228 pounds a year. Ten thousand eagles would therefore consume annually 2,280,000 pounds, and that is the estimated maximum that they collect from the desert scrub, the grasslands, and the crags of West Texas. What the actual destruction is among various types of prey, no one knows for sure. There are about 10 million sheep and goats in West Texas on open range. If half of this figure is made up of lambs and kids, and if the eagles take as many lambs or kids as the ranchers claim, they would be losing 15,000 a year. That would be .3 percent of the yearly crop.

The chief complainants are the sheep and goat men, although the cattlemen are often their spokesmen. Yet the case against the golden eagle when it comes to calves is practically nil, for the only proved cases are instances where golden eagles have eaten the carrion of still-born calves.

The usual foods of the golden eagle are insects, reptiles, large rodents, rabbits, marmots, ground squirrels, and sometimes grouse and ptarmigan. There is no doubt that the golden eagle does take kids from flocks of goats and antelope fawns. I know that from my own researches in the Pacific West. There is no doubt that they will sometimes take a lamb. But the practice is not common or widespread. Montana studies show, for example, that golden eagles do not prey on sheep even in the sheep areas.

The eagle, of course, has competitors in this forage for food, chief among which are other hawks, the mountain lion, the bobcat, the coyote, and the fox. This group over the centuries adjusted themselves to the available food, and in their wintering grounds these predators spread out into enough territory to be in adjustment with the quantity of their prey.

This predatory population did not deplete the prey. If it had done so, the prey would not be here today. The arrival of cattle, sheep, and goats increased the category of available prey, but there is very little evidence that eagles kill substantial amounts of lambs, kids, or antelope fawn.

My studies led me to favor the Audubon Society. And so does Peter Koch of Alpine, Texas, who is one of our foremost experts on the golden eagle. When he moved to West Texas from Ohio after World War II, he became absorbed in studying the golden eagle. He sought out its nests, built scaffolds he could lower from cliffs to viewpoints where he could observe it in its habitat. He found three nesting places in the Chisos Mountains and from precarious perches took movies of these birds, producing a full-length lecture film. Hunters hired by ranchers were exterminating them very fast; Peter found one nest where both parents had been shot, leaving a fledgling. He managed to rescue this chick and raised it to maturity. He was the food provider for it, trapping rabbits and mice, the main diet of the golden eagle, and presenting them to his ward. The bird grew to maturity under Peter's tender care and was quite tame, coming at his call. But in time a deeper instinct took hold and he disappeared.

"Perhaps he was so tame he was easily shot," Peter adds wistfully.

However that may be, Peter Koch maintains that the killer of lambs, so hated by the ranchers, is the ferruginous rough-leg hawk (*Buteo ragalis*). This bird has a snowy-white undersurface (though no dark terminal band). So the golden eagle could easily be mistaken for it by any but the most sophisticated bird watcher.

The *Presidio Voice*, published in Presidio, Texas, had another theory that also acquits the golden eagle. It wrote in August 1966:

> Now about the American Eagle whom the Texas ranchers claim they are killing their little goats and sheeps, as a matter of fact

I think the Governor must give this matter further consideration before signing a law to give permission to the Ranchers to kill the Eagles. This matter should be investigated and closely be on watch of the sheep and goat herders, probably they are the ones that are stealing the kids and baby lambs. We advise— be on watch! You can't trust people now a day, due to high cost of living.

The ranchers believe that the Big Bend National Park is a reservoir for golden eagles who use it as headquarters and make sorties out of it to prey on livestock. But the Big Bend, though large to the human eye, is not large enough to accommodate even a small fraction of the region's winter eagle population; and probably no golden eagles nest there any more.

Walter R. Spofford's study for the Audubon Society in 1963 states the basic facts. He traveled 7,000 miles by truck and spent 31 hours in the air studying the golden eagle.

The golden eagle migrates from Alaska, the Pacific West, and the mountain regions to Central Mexico and West Texas. But the golden eagle population is thinly spread over vast areas, each breeding pair occupying a territory from 25 to 100 square miles in which various nests are used in rotation.

Eagles living in Mexico and West Texas do not migrate, as they have a permanent food supply. Farther north the golden eagle depends on prey species that hibernate in the winter. Most Northern golden eagles start south in the fall when their food supply declines. It is this migrant population that is the larger part of the eagle population in West Texas. When they were killed in what became a notorious "winter shoot-off," the national census drastically dropped. The "winter shoot-off" became possible when the ranchers in 1937 got Austin officials to take the golden eagle from the list of birds protected by Texas law.

The hunter by plane sometimes used a 12-gauge shotgun with pistol grip and recoil spring mounted on a frame outside the

fuselage. The plane followed the eagle up six, seven, eight thousand feet or more. The airplane hunters say there is just one minute as the plane flies up behind an eagle which is perfect for shooting, for the eagle may quickly circle up and, if he hits a thermal updraft, will outfly the plane. But eagles who have been shot at learn to drop quickly toward the ground, for then they can seldom be shot from the air. With an eagle moving 40 miles an hour and a small plane 50, there is a good chance of hitting it in flight. But with an eagle flying low, a descent close enough to the ground for an accurate shot is too dangerous. Other hunters by plane used a 12-gauge shotgun hand-held, flying up behind the eagle. The pilot opened a window and shot from the shoulder.

The "winter shoot-off" of eagles by airplanes was practiced by pilots at five or more airports in West Texas.

Thousands of golden eagles were shot, one pilot alone killing 1,200 in West Texas in one year. The gravity of that offense is appreciated in reference to the total population of the golden eagle—west, east, north, and south. That total population is probably 8,000 or perhaps 10,000. And the breeding population is only from 2,000 to 3,000 pairs, as golden eagles do not breed until they are five years old, and not every year after that. The winter population of golden eagles in Mexico and West Texas, including migrants, is probably 5,000 or 6,000.

Spofford estimates that as a result of the use of the airplane and the regular "winter shoot-off" about 20,000 golden eagles were killed in West Texas in the last 20 years. J. O. Casparis of Alpine gives the total between 1941 and 1947 as 4,818 golden eagles.

The size of the shoot-off was comparable to that of the estimated yearly crop of juvenile eagles. The fact that the eagle population has not dropped to extremely low levels is due to the fact that this bird is basically long-lived, and the effect of the shoot-off takes longer to become manifest. A shoot-off of a local predator population may have an immediate effect as with coyotes or mountain lions, but a shoot-off of migratory birds may drain half a continent without any immediate perceptible local effect. Several times as many eagles have to be shot as make up the local population at any one time because replacements arrive. Spofford estimates that to reduce a population of 1,000 eagles to 200 eagles in West Texas, some 3,000 eagles would have to be killed during the winter. As he concludes, "This is an incredibly wasteful procedure."

Park officials think there are no golden eagles left in the Big Bend area. Spofford found none. He saw some in the Davis Mountains, along the Valentine Plain, and above the flats out of Marfa where the grass crop is fair. He found few in the areas of dry desert scrub.

Eagles are easy to spot from a plane. Spofford on a three-hour flight in the Davis Mountains area covered 200 square miles and saw six at widely scattered points. On another flight covering 1,000 square miles he saw eight. On another 10-hour flight that covered 600 miles of linear flight over an area several thousand square miles large he spotted 33.

The golden eagle population in West Texas as we entered the 1960s was indeed thin.

The Congress in 1940 had taken steps to protect the bald eagle (54 Stat. 250). In 1962 the Congress undertook to protect the golden eagle as well (76 Stat. 1246). The statute provides: "Whenever, after investigation, the Secretary of the Interior shall determine" that the taking of the bald eagle or golden eagle is "necessary" for "the protection of wild life or of agricultural or other interests in any particular locality, he may authorize the taking of such eagles pursuant to regulations which he is hereby authorized to prescribe: *Provided,* That on request of the Governor of any State, the Secretary of the Interior shall authorize the taking of golden eagles for the purpose of seasonally protecting domesticated flocks and herds in such State, in accordance with regulations established under the provisions of this section, in such part or parts of such State and for such periods as the Secretary determines to be necessary to protect such interests."

By regulations the Secretary banned the taking of golden eagles "by poison or from aircraft," though he allowed their taking under permit "by firearms, traps, or other suitable means." (50 C.F.R. § 11.4.) The Regulations also provide:

> The Secretary may issue permits to take bald eagles or golden eagles when he determines they have become seriously injurious to wild life or to agricultural or other interests in any particular area in the United States or in any place subject to its jurisdiction, and the injury complained of is substantial and can be abated only by taking some or all of the offending birds.
>
> Whenever the Governor of any State requests permission to take golden eagles to seasonally protect livestock, the Secretary will authorize such taking without a permit in whatever part or parts of the State and for such periods as he determines necessary to protect those interests.
>
> No bald eagle may be taken for any purpose unless, prior to such taking a permit to do so has been issued by the Secretary. (50 C.F.R. § 11.3.)

Permits have been issued by Secretary Udall as follows:

Year Issued	Control Period
1963	January 10 – April 30, 1963
1963	December 16, 1963 – April 30, 1964
1964	December 15, 1964 – June 15, 1965
1965	December 15, 1965 – June 15, 1966

Since the young hatch in March and are out of the nest by early June, the foregoing periods cover the entire nesting period of the golden eagle. "These permits will destroy completely every resident bird," Peter Koch sadly observed.

The authorization to take golden eagles without permit has been extended to 32 counties in Texas:

El Paso	Ward	Sutton	Tom Green
Jeff Davis	Upton	Pecos	Coke
Brewster	Hudspeth	Culbertson	Scheicher
Val Verde	Presidio	Real	Crane
Uvalde	Terrell	Sterling	Burnet
Kerr	Kinney	Glasscock	McCulloch
Edwards	Bandera	Reagan	Blanco
Crockett	Kimble	Irion	San Saba

The conditions under which golden eagles may be taken as stipulated in the authorization signed by Secretary Udall are as follows:

1. Golden eagles may be taken without a permit only for the protection of domesticated livestock and only by livestock owners and their agents.

2. Golden eagles may be taken by any suitable means or methods except by the use of poison or from aircraft.

3. Golden eagles or any parts thereof taken pursuant to this authorization may not be possessed, purchased, sold, traded, bartered, or offered for sale, trade, or barter.

4. Any person taking golden eagles pursuant to this authorization must at all reasonable times, including during actual operations, permit any Federal or state game agent or deputy game agent, warden, protector, or other game-law-enforcement officer, free and unrestricted access over the premises on which such operations have been or are being conducted; and shall furnish promptly to such officer whatever information he may require concerning such operations.

Eagles are shot when circling low. They are also caught by

placing traps on dead sheep or deer. The annual toll continues. Before aerial shooting was banned, more than 1,000 golden eagles were killed yearly in the Southwest. That number has dropped materially. But in Texas alone it is estimated that hundreds are taken yearly under Secretary Udall's permit system.

We were talking about these problems of the golden eagle in Alpine—Justice Jim, Peter Koch, and Dr. Barton Warnock of Sul Ross College. We debated the pros and cons of the ranchers' complaint against this magnificent bird. Dr. Warnock brought the whole discussion into ecological focus by saying: "We know that West Texas land is too heavily pounded by sheep and goats. If an eagle takes a lamb or a kid it is protecting the land by helping restore the balance." He added, "Should eagles or any other predator for that matter reduce any rancher's sheep crop by half, most likely he still would be overstocked."

I left Alpine on that trip thinking that Dr. Warnock was right: that we too often resent Nature's way of protecting our resources. Spofford said the same thing in his report:

"The slaughter of eagles and other predators is the ultimate phase in an attempt to harvest the last sheep and goat crop in a dying land."

John H. Storer talks about this ecological problem in *The Web of Life*. Living things are dynamic, always trying to expand. When population grows in an area so as to menace the food supply, predators move in; and when their prey is reduced, the predators die off or move to other areas. Storer illustrates the problem by considering soil bacteria, the smallest and simplest of all living things. Under favorable conditions each individual would divide into two about twice every hour. Even if it happened only once in an hour, the offspring from a single individual would number 17 million in a day, and by the end of six days the cells would have increased to a bulk larger than the earth.

West Texas is heavily overstocked, the experts saying that if half the animals were removed, there would still be too many. But biologists and ecologists get short shrift in West Texas.

"This is my land, isn't it?"

"I can do what I like with it, can't I?"

"Every eagle must be shot. Let me ask you, Mr. Justice, would you stand by and let predators eat half of your capital investment?"

Many West Texans have little appreciation of the responsibility of man to the earth. They pound it to pieces and curse anyone or anything, including the golden eagle, that stands in the way.

But as Don McIvor said when we saw the eagles circling on Mount Livermore, "Every time they take a sheep or goat they're doing the rancher a favor though he may not know it."

The golden eagle, a great and glorious part of our inheritance, is part of Naboth's vineyard that Ahabs wearing sombreros are appropriating for their own selfish purposes.

CHAPTER IX

THE GUADALUPES

The Guadalupes are a rugged mountain range west of the Pecos River in West Texas that extends north into New Mexico. They are the exposed part of the Capitan Reef, a limestone formation that was built under water when the ocean lay over this land, and later elevated. Most of the reef is underground in New Mexico. Near its southern edge is Guadalupe Peak, which rises 8,751 feet, the highest point in Texas. As one moves north and northwesterly into New Mexico, the Capitan Reef becomes less elevated, the western escarpment being only 3,650 feet high. El Capitan, an isolated, towering, column-shaped mountain, is the southernmost point of the Capitan Reef.

U.S. Highway 62 and 180 passes not far south of El Capitan, and one who travels it can see from Guadalupe Pass, a few miles south of Pine Springs, the sheer cliffs of this mountain. They are so steep that they have never been climbed, and they are so treacherous they may never be. The top of El Capitan has been reached by climbing one of the canyons such as Bear Canyon on the east side of the range, going to the top of Guadalupe Peak, and then dropping down to the top of El Capitan.

El Capitan was the landmark for the early travelers. The old

Butterfield Overland Mail ran beneath it, and the remains of one of its pineries are still visible. Airplane pilots from the beginning have used El Capitan as an all-weather outpost for navigation. In the winter it is not uncommon for heavy fog to lie thick on the land to the east of the Guadalupes and curl softly around the base of El Capitan. One of the most magnificent views I have seen is El Capitan rising above this long, thick finger of desert fog.

Early chronicles reported seeing El Capitan and its companion, Guadalupe Peak, for days on end. Those who traveled by ox train reported that they could see it "for a week or more and never seem to get near it."

John R. Bartlett stated the matter as follows:

> The Guadalupes had been before us the whole day, and we all expected to reach it within a couple of hours after leaving camp. But hour after hour we drove directly toward it, without seeming to approach nearer; and finally, after journeying 10 hours, the mountain seemed to be as distant as it was in the morning. Such is the great clearness of the atmosphere here, that one unused to measuring distances in elevated regions is greatly deceived. When this mountain was first discovered we were more than 100 miles off. Even then its features stood out boldly against the blue sky; and when the rays of the morning sun were shed upon it, it exhibited every outline of its rugged sides with as much distinctness as a similar object would in the old states at one-fifth the distance. Often have I gazed upon the Kattskill Mountains in sailing down the Hudson; and though at a distance of but 12 miles, I never saw them as distinctly as the Guadalupe mountain appeared 60 miles off.

W. L. Ormsby, reporter from the *New York Herald,* in the 1880s, wrote as he viewed El Capitan that "it seems as if Nature had saved up all her ruggedness to pile it up in this colossal form."

Frank X. Tolbert of the Dallas *Morning News* calls El Capitan

"one of the biggest exposed fossil reefs in the world"; and he adds that the sun in the morning and late afternoon makes "gorgeous dyes on its yellow face."

The first historic references to the Guadalupes were in the journals of Spanish conquistadors who journeyed north from Mexico; their expeditions were not into the Guadalupes but around them on the northwest side. An American expedition headed by Lieut. Francis Bryan in 1849 passed along the base of the Guadalupes. Capt. J. Polk surveyed for a railroad through this area in 1854. Then came the Butterfield Overland trail, and with it, pinery at the mouth of Pine Spring Canyon.

After the Civil War, ranchers settled along the base of the escarpment in some of the canyons. But the highest reaches of the Guadalupes were immune from much grazing by reason of the lack of water.

Indians lived in the Guadalupes. We know this from excavations made in a few of the cave sites which have been weathered out of the limestone cliffs. These were not casual nor recent occupancies. Some went back 6,000 years, one at least more than 12,000 years. Pottery has been obtained that dates back approximately 600 years. The latest inhabitants were probably the Mescalero Apaches, who resided there when the white settlers first came. Until the Apaches arrived, apparently no crops were raised, and there is no evidence of masonry structures. In the beginning the Indians were gatherers and hunters, living in caves and under the overhangs in the limestone cliffs. They apparently used outdoor kitchens of the roasting-pit type. These pits are found at all elevations, indicating the Indians followed the ripening of the plants from the valley floor in the spring to the highest reaches in the fall.

The caves of the Guadalupes show many pictographs. But most of the archaeological work yet remains to be done.

Some of the most provocative work in the Guadalupes has

been done by amateurs—the late William Barnett and W. H. Balgemann of Carlsbad, New Mexico. I spent time with the latter and caught some of his enthusiasm. The archaeology of the Guadalupes is his hobby and he has absorbed much from first-hand excavations and from his work with the experts.

He groups these ancient people as follows:

> 25000 B.C. to 15000 B.C.—Mid Paleo Indian
> 15000 B.C. to 7000 B.C.—Late Paleo Indian
> 7000 B.C. to 3000 B.C.—Early Guadalupian Cave
>   Dwelling Basket Makers
> 3000 B.C. to 1000 B.C.—Mid Guadalupian Cave
>   Dwelling Basket Makers
> 1000 B.C. to A.D. 1400—Late Guadalupian Cave
>   Dwelling Basket Makers
> A.D. 1400 to A.D. 1900—Mescalero and Lipan Apache
>   Indians (nomadic groups)

The Guadalupes were once under water in an estuary of the sea comprising some 10,000 square miles and called the Delaware Basin. It was roughly oval in shape, with a channel to the open ocean to the southwest. The Capitan Reef was a massive bed in that basin. It extended in the form of a giant horseshoe 350 to 400 miles around the Basin's margin. Lime-secreting algae were chiefly responsible for the growth of this barrier; and other organisms contributed their corpses to the structure and aided in trapping and holding a limey sand in the growing deposits. Except for its oval shape, the Capitan Reef is similar to present-day barrier reefs that are exposed in the Pacific.

Associated with the Capitan Reef are thickly bedded, steeply dipping rocks which represent re-crystallized talus slopes, built forward in comparatively deep water and advancing in front of the margin of the Capitan Reef. The growth of the Capitan Reef was more in a horizontal than vertical direction, and the

Reef apparently grew largely on its own talus. Large blocks of rock which slid down the slopes in front of the Reef were incorporated in the basin deposits. These sub-marine slides are very much on display in the Guadalupes. Behind the Capitan Reef in the lagoonal area several types of sediments, known as back-reef equivalents, accumulated. They consist primarily of dolomite with an interbedding of fine-grained sandstone.

The geologists emphasize this remarkable display of deep-water basin deposits of reef talus, and of shallow-water sediments, all formed at the same time by different causes in the environments from which they originate. They indeed get excited over these geological phenomena.

What Texas has in the Guadalupes is, geologically speaking, one of the great wonders of the world. It takes the trained eye to analyze all this, but even the untrained eye can see glories resplendent, and with the help of an observer as acute as Peter Koch, the layman can begin to see and understand things of which he never dreamed.

The underworld of the Capitan Reef is also wondrous to behold. One sees it best in the Carlsbad Caverns National Park, not far from Carlsbad, New Mexico. Here the ground is 4,406 feet above sea level. The main cavern in that 47,000-acre national park is only one of many limestone caves in the Capitan Reef. Nearly 600,000 people a year find it fascinating.

The cave, which drops as low as 1,013 feet below the earth's surface, has nearly three miles of surfaced trails, all lighted. Below the main cavern—some eight miles in length—is another one as yet open only to special guests. The temperature in the cavern remains at approximately 56° F. the year round whether there is zero weather outside or 100° F. The dissolving action of underground water has worked wonders, producing some formations as delicate as needles and others in the form of massive chandeliers. Once solution holes were formed, dripping water, holding minute quantities of dissolved limestone, came through the ceilings. Exposed to the air, these droplets evaporated and left their mineral content (calcite and aragonite) as crystalline forms of limestone. Over the centuries this slow process of evaporation and deposition built a myriad of crystalline stalactites of infinite variety of shapes and sizes; and the process still continues. Also, water dripping to the floor built numerous stalagmites in like fashion. Stalactites and stalagmites joined together to become columns or pillars. There are also twisted formations called helicites that seem to defy gravity in their growth.

The caverns contain some wild life—a ringtail cat, some mice, and a noiseless cricket. But most spectacular of all is the Mexican free-tail bat that frequents undeveloped sections of the caverns by the hundreds of thousands. Each summer evening around sunset thousands of them spiral upward out of the cavern entrance and fly southward to the Black and Pecos River basins for feeding. Their guano was once commercially exploited here.

Four of North America's seven climatic life zones are present in the Guadalupes: Lower Sonoran in the lower canyons; Upper Sonoran on the ridges; Transition in shaded draws and on canyon floors; Canadian on the highest points.

Huge, yawning canyons have been cut into the sides of this range—Bear, South McKittrick, and North McKittrick on the east and East Dog Canyon and West Dog Canyon on the west.

We climbed the Guadalupes, muleback, going up Bear Canyon, a steep, rocky gorge where limestone caves show the weathering of centuries.

We started at Frijole, once the highest-altitude post office in Texas. Noel Kincaid, our guide, is its present justice of the peace, administering what Frank X. Tolbert calls "The Law West of the Pecos." Noel, thinking I was a justice of the peace, was amazed at my ignorance when I did not know any of his judicial colleagues in West Texas. As Tolbert says, Frijole is "a

clutch of stone, adobe, frame buildings, and high corrals around a spring of sweet water." The mules, according to Noel Kincaid, have "mountain lungs" and most of us rode them rather than horses. From Frijole the eastern slopes seem impassable even to mules. The ascent is steep, perhaps 40 degrees or more. But the anatomy of each square yard shows safe footing, and we made it without incident.

The Guadalupes, rising out of the Chihuahua Desert, give man in a short space of a few miles the contrast between a desert climate and one such as southern Canada's. The temperature at the top is 20 degrees lower than at the bottom. The 25 to 30 inches of rain on top is double that (or more) of the precipitation on the surrounding flats.

At the top we rested in a great gale out of the northwest. I sat on the escarpment looking eastward from whence we had come. Far to the southeast are the Delaware Mountains. In between is a flat basin overlaid with gypsum (some of it red) that, prior to paved roads, was churned into a fine dust by wagons and automobiles. I felt momentarily that I was in the center of the Anti-Lebanon Mountains looking east toward Baghdad. I said as much; and Mickey Burleson, expressing doubts, said, "Sure nuff?" And as I nodded, J. C. Hunter, Jr., who then owned much of the Guadalupes, asked, Texas style, "How come?"

I explained that except for the oasis of Damascus, the land east of the Anti-Lebanon is dry scrub land; and so is the land at the foot of the Guadalupes in West Texas. As far as the eye can see, it is desolate desert land filled with greasewood, sotol, and yucca. From the rim of Bear Canyon these details are missing; only grays and browns appear with dark lines where the grease-wood streaks across the rolling plain. But the scene is strikingly similar to the one east of the Anti-Lebanon Mountains and filled me with a nostalgia. The Anti-Lebanon Mountains are also limestone. They, too, are worn by water and other abrasives into strange shapes. The limestone and the distant desert are indeed a replica of that part of the Middle East.

When I mentioned these matters, Peter Koch went on to explain the transformation that has taken place in these West Texas lands since he first arrived in the 1940s. Pointing with his finger toward Valentine and Van Horn and drawing a big circle, he described how rich the land once was in grass. First came the cattle, and their overcrowding made the land suffer. Forage enough for sheep and goats, but not enough for cattle, remained. So, greedy man turned those rapacious animals loose and they literally tore out the roots of the grass, bearing witness to John Muir's dictum, "As sheep advance, flowers, vegetation, grass, soil, plenty, and poetry vanish."

"Instead of grass we now have desert," said Peter Koch. "And it will take eons of time to bring any grass back."

A three-inch metal pipe line keeps close to the trail all the way up Bear Canyon and empties into a large iron tank at the top. The pipe brings water to the highlands from a bounteous clear spring in the valley that runs 20 gallons per minute, a water hole marked Upper Pine Spring on the map. J. C. Hunter, Jr., installed the line, carrying pipe through New Mexico to the top of the Guadalupes and along jeep roads to the brink of Bear Canyon, where it was lowered section by section and the pieces welded by a crew who worked their way downhill. This water is the only water on top of the Guadalupes, except runoff water caught in natural potholes or collected by Mr. Hunter behind earthen dams. But there are no creeks, no springs, no rivers on top of the Guadalupes, in spite of the fact that limestone is an excellent cistern.

In the canyons there is an abundance of water for game, and deer and elk travel considerable distances to them when a drought reaches the crest of the Guadalupes. The parallel with the Anti-Lebanon is perfect. For the latter also hold an abundance of moisture that collects underground to form the Barrada River, which fairly leaps out of a bungalow-size cave to run some 50 miles to Damascus—an oasis kept green and lush by it.

We turned from the escarpment and walked west a few dozen yards to enter a thick conifer forest. This forest extends a couple miles, filling what is known as the Bowl. It is a relic forest such as the ones in the Chisos and Davis Mountains. This one is predominantly Douglas fir and ponderosa pine, with a scattering of juniper, Gambel's oak, and madrone trees, together with an occasional aspen. This forest took hold here perhaps in Pleistocene times—at least eons ago when the rainfall was great. It reproduced through the centuries, and is still reproducing. The ponderosa is not quite as "yellow bellied" as ours in the Pacific West. Nor is it or the Douglas fir so gargantuan in growth or height as the Pacific species. But they are not dwarf or stunted. They are indeed patricians in their own class.

This day they were especially magnificent. A great gale was

blowing from the northwest; and once I approached the forest I could hear the orchestration of the conifers. John Muir used to climb the pines in Yosemite during storms, sit in their crests as they swung a wide arc, and listen to their music. I did not climb the Douglas fir or the ponderosa in the Bowl. But I sat at their feet in adoration. A high wind sets up a vibration in every needle. Thus, each branch seems to be alive with little dancers; and their movement produces a low hum. The waving of the branches sets up a louder beat. And above them all comes a slower one when the whole tree creaks backward and forward. This is for me the supreme excitement of the pines and fir forest. Never have I heard an orchestration of strings that could equal the one produced on the Guadalupes this cold, bright morning.

The top of the Guadalupes is a composite of brush, ridges, and peaks. It is sparsely wooded, apart from the Bowl itself. It is ideal riding country, where one in the saddle seems to be on top of the world with an almost limitless expanse in every direction. The woods are open, the sun bright, the air cool. This is heaven to one who likes adventure, on foot or horseback. Canyons drop off on both the west and east sides, the most luxurious being eastward flowing; and of these, South McKittrick is the most exciting, as we shall see. As one travels in a northerly direction toward New Mexico the vegetation becomes sparse. Nowhere are there massive displays of flowers. Coming up Bear Canyon we saw an occasional yellow poppy, a few scattered phlox, and here and there a bright blue flax. On top we saw over and over again the Indian paintbrush, but never in beds. The century plant is thick, and the more open slopes north of the Bowl have much sotol and yucca with scatterings of juniper and piñon pine. In between the Bowl and the more open northern country are a few velvet ash (*Fraximus velutina*). What at a distance I thought were wild cherries in bloom turned out on

close examination to be the serviceberry. The scant bloom of
the serviceberry gave a delicate touch to the monotones of the
transition forest.

There is only one trail over the top that commences and ends
on the east side, and that is the one we took up Bear Canyon.
It comes out right close to the J. C. Hunter Lodge in South
McKittrick Canyon; but the arc it travels takes about nine hours
to traverse by horse. After it leaves the Bowl it drops down to
the head of South McKittrick Canyon and then climbs again to
open land slick with outcroppings of limestone and thick with
scrub. From this point we could see New Mexico to the north,
the Del City irrigation project to the south, and the vast, rolling
Chihuahua Desert to the east. The trail is a tortuous one that
J. C. Hunter, Jr.'s father built years ago to accommodate hunting parties. After climbing out of South McKittrick it keeps to
the rim, which is a rough, undulating ridge where either a horse
or a man on foot must pick his way with care. Along this rim
we saw ancient fire holes of sotol burners. There is a high sugar
content in the thorny leaves of this plant; and Indians and other
border people used these fire holes to distill a 190-proof alcohol
from the plant. The trail, after circling the rim, drops down a
precipitous hogback too steep to ride; and then it climbs again
at a 60-degree pitch. After that it skirts the north face of a cliff
so that one on horseback looks down a thousand feet or more,
almost sheer, not realizing his horse is walking a platform made
from drilling holes in the stone wall into which iron rods have
been inserted. The trail is indeed made of logs and dirt laid on
top of the iron rods, the logs being laced in place with bailing
wire.

Traveling this trail took me back in memory to a journey
into Hunza in the northern part of West Pakistan. The Karako-
rams often provide precipitous cliffs where no pathway can be
found. It was customary in ancient times to make a trail by

wedging sticks into cracks across the face of a cliff and then lacing brush to these sticks to make a thick surface. I once saw mules make that dangerous traverse; and I, too, walked gingerly across one. But I never relished that encounter with disaster any more than I did the day I traversed the narrow catwalk that protrudes from the side of the sheer cliff above McKittrick Canyon.

After a few hundred yards, however, we regained the ridge, off of which a precipitous serpentine trail, too steep for riding, drops, drops, drops 2,000 feet or more.

Early on this trip we had "mule trouble." Jack Long, a television cameraman from Houston, rode a little mule appropriately called Wino. Wino behaved beautifully on the climb up Bear Canyon, but when he reached the top he threw Jack Long. By then the caravan was ahead, but Jack managed to get aboard only to be thrown again. This time Wino ran furiously down the trail trying to catch up with the rest of the caravan. Noel Kincaid, who was waiting for stragglers, caught the fugitive mule and tied him in some nearby bushes where he could not be seen. In a little time Jack Long came running down the trail asking, "Did anyone see my mule?"

"He must have gone somewhere else," said Noel Kincaid.

And after letting Jack Long worry a good long Texas 10 minutes, Noel brought Wino out of hiding. Shortly, Wino threw Jack Long again, going high in the air, twisting his body, and coming down hard on four feet. Long, with his heavy camera, survived eight leaps and then landed heavily on his head and suffered a mild concussion.

"Now, don't go and get mule fever," said Noel Kincaid. "Got one man up here so scared that he would not come down either on foot or horseback. Had to send a truck clear up to New Mexico on a jeep road to pack him out."

Once we came to the precipitous slope where the trail drops 2,000 feet more, Wino acted like a gentleman, as mules do when danger is near. It was on this slope that Noel Kincaid had recently traveled with his favorite mule. He dismounted to lead his mule over the treacherous path and soon came to a rough section of the trail where he had to step up a foot under the overhang of the limestone cliff. The mule followed; but it jumped a little too high so that the horn of the saddle hit the cliff, knocking the mule off balance. Noel Kincaid, thinking quickly, tossed the reins to the mule, who made a jump into outer space, dropping into brush 50 feet below. Noel thought the mule was dead. It took 15 minutes for Noel to reach the animal, and when he arrived, he found him peacefully chewing on bunch grass.

"A few experiences like that," Noel said, "and a fellow would git good mule disease."

This portion is too rough for any animals except deer or bighorn.

"A tough place to look for a cow," I told Noel.

"You'd never find one."

The last two miles have gentler slopes. We found wild cherries in bloom, a rattlesnake coiled on a rock, and a cold, purling creek filled with trout, and at the bottom we found steak and hot biscuits prepared by Noel Kincaid, who was not too tired after nine hours in the saddle to be the cook.

J. C. Hunter, Jr., ran Brangus cattle in the Guadalupes, a cross between the Brahmas and the Black Angus, and goats, too. But Mr. Hunter, unlike most West Texas ranchers, fenced them out of the choice places.

No livestock grazed South McKittrick Canyon and the high country of the Guadalupes, including the Bowl. The range animals used East Dog Canyon, West Dog Canyon, the Frijole Area, and the foothill area west of the main escarpment. As a result of these controls, the delicate balance which the ecology of this desert-alpine area demands has been maintained in the choice scenic spots.

Elk have been introduced, and they possess the Bowl. They

were imported in the 1920s and have prospered, the herd now being about 100 strong. Once the native elk (*Cervus merriami*) roamed here. Now it is the *Cervus canadensis nelsoni*. The hunting was good; J. C. Hunter, Jr., took his guests in over the steep Bear Canyon trail we climbed. Mule deer are also present and they are plentiful, the large ones dressing down to 200 pounds. The desert bighorn sheep once roamed there. And a ram or two was seen in the early sixties. But the herd is now extinct. Some of the bighorn sheep in the Guadalupes apparently left that range and crossed over to the Sierra Diablo to the south—a range that has awesome canyons and wild reaches as rugged as any I know. I visited J. V. McAdoo at his 55-section ranch in those mountains and saw the bighorn trophies he has collected. The last head was taken in 1935 and, according to Mr. McAdoo, the last of the Sierra Diablo bighorns died in 1945. The cause, according to him, was disease. "Domestic sheep moved in on all sides of the Sierra Diablo and mixed with the bighorns who had no immunity from common sheep diseases and died like flies."

The Guadalupes once had the native Merriam turkey, but it disappeared years ago. In 1954 turkeys of the same species were introduced from New Mexico, and by the 1960s they had increased to a flock of about 200.

The Guadalupes have some mountain lions and a few black bear, bobcats, ringtails, raccoons, skunks, coyote, gray fox, porcupine, rock squirrels, and rabbits (both jack and cottontail).

We know from archaeological studies that, in addition to the original native elk, the Taylor bison also occupied the Guadalupes, as did the four-horned antelope, the musk ox, and a species of the early horse.

Plans were afoot for several years to make the Guadalupes a national park. A public-spirited Texan, Wallace Pratt, started the ball rolling by giving the Federal government 6,000 acres at the mouths of South McKittrick and North McKittrick canyons.

Mr. Hunter was willing to sell his vast acreage at a reasonable price.

Texas has no more important shrine than the towering Guadalupes. They can be an eternal blessing to untold thousands of outdoor enthusiasts. The objection to preserving them came not from Texans but from the Texas officialdom. Some wanted the Guadalupes for the oil interests. Mr. Pratt and Mr. Hunter, both oilmen, wanted the Guadalupes saved for posterity. But the powers-that-be wanted to despoil the unique narrow canyons

with roads, and try to convert the rocks of the Guadalupes into dollars.

Some of the modern Ahabs destroying Texas sit in the seats of the mighty in Austin, the capital. Others throughout Texas wanted the national park and were willing to waive the mineral claims that Texas had. Senator Ralph W. Yarborough rallied the forces of conservation and finally got a bill passed creating the Guadalupe Mountains National Park, Texas (80 Stat. 920), which the President approved October 15, 1966. The conservationists hopefully believe that this high escarpment, unique in the Southwest, will now be available throughout the centuries for refugees from the hot Chihuahua Desert. Whether they will be disillusioned remains to be seen, for some modern Ahabs wear Federal uniforms and sit in the seats of the mighty in Washington, D.C.

CHAPTER X

THE McKITTRICK CANYONS
AND ON NORTH

Highway 62 from El Paso east is today modern in every respect but it follows what was known in ancient days as the Salt Road. It is still long and monotonous with little habitation. Not much rain falls, and the little that does, evaporates. Here along the highway may be seen salt flats where for ages water evaporation has left a salt residue. Near these salt flats and along Highway 54 out of Van Horn are quite a few salt lakes, some of considerable size, where human beings may float like a cork. Route 180 from Pine Springs to El Paso bisects another of those salt lakes just west of Salt Lake, Texas. One of these is indeed known as the Great Salt Lake. Salt was taken from time immemorial out of this salt basin and not only used by the Indians who frequented the area, but transported by them into Mexico through the town of San Elizario near El Paso.

With the increasing settlement of West Texas, the trade became so important that a road from San Elizario to the salt flats was built and that was the road known as Salt Road.

It was around these salt lakes that the Salt War waged.

There is in San Elizario an old mission church built in 1682, once a part of the convent brought into prominence by a red-haired señorita whose hand was sought by two men.

One version of the war is that in 1877 they competed for this red-haired señorita. This rivalry led to armed conflict. One was shot in El Paso and the other by an indignant mob in San Elizario.

But the essence of the Salt Lake War was quite different. The story runs as follows and is related in Gillett, *Six Years with the Texas Rangers* (1943).

It seems that for 100 years or more the residents along the Rio Grande on both sides of the river hauled salt from the salt lakes free of charge, paying no one, as the land was in the public domain. It was a long, dreary haul from these salt lakes to San Elizario, some 90 miles without any water. The salt haulers carried water in barrels to what was known as the Half-Way Station. There they would rest and water their horses, leaving some of their supplies for the return trip.

A man by the name of Charles Howard was elected judge in El Paso in the 1870s. He saw the possibilities of these salt lakes as commercial enterprises and, knowing they were on public land, arranged to file on them. When the filings were complete, he forbade anyone to haul salt from the lakes without first securing his permission. The people on both sides of the Rio Grande, especially the Mexicans, became highly indignant. A man who carried overland mail between El Paso and Fort Davis, by the name of Luis Cardis, took the side of the haulers of salt, making him a bitter enemy of Howard.

In September, 1878, Howard shot Cardis in El Paso. This precipitated the Salt Lake War. Howard asked the Governor of Texas to send Texas Rangers to protect him and the court over which he presided. The Texas Rangers made the long overland trip of 750 miles from San Antonio. The Mexicans outwitted the head of the Texas Rangers, captured him, disarmed the Rangers, took possession of Howard and other Americans aligned with him, lined them up against an adobe wall and shot them. Then they placed a rope around Howard's neck and mounting on fast ponies dragged the body around the streets of San Elizario. Relief forces arrived but the murderers of Howard had scattered and none of them was ever apprehended and tried for the crime.

Another to lose his life in the conflict was Kid McKittrick, and it is for McKittrick that McKittrick Canyon has been named. But what his real connection with the Guadalupes was, is lost in history.

A dirt road winds for several miles across scrubby desert land toward the mouth of the two McKittrick canyons. Just before one comes to the point of land that divides South from North McKittrick, he comes to a giant juniper tree whose bark has been peeled off on the eastern side and whose wood has been beveled by an ax. If one gets down on his knees, he will see three handmade square nails in a row in the wood of the juniper, very close to the ground. The legend is that a cave containing lost gold lies in a direct line that one sights along the three nails. There are indeed several caves that are possible targets of this trajectory and some people have made preliminary explorations of them, but no gold has yet been discovered.

There are many legends of a lost gold mine in the Guadalupes. The Spaniards were said to have been shown a large gold deposit on the east spurs of the Guadalupes by an Indian. Geronimo, notorious leader of the Apaches, is reported as saying that the largest gold mine in the world lay hidden in the Guadalupes. In the 1880s Ben Sublett, a prospector from Odessa, used to go into a cave somewhere on the mountain, returning with nuggets. Sublett never told the location of the mine. Ben Watson, a prospector still alive at the age of one hundred, says he knows where the mine is, but won't tell because "the world isn't ready for that time yet." Frank Dobie wrote about the mine in his book *Coronado's Children.*

As I have said, there are two McKittrick canyons—North and

South. The North one has a little water and some rare botanical species, one being a pink rose (*R. stellata*), commonly known as the desert rose.

The most interesting canyon is the South one. It is scenically more rugged; and it has in four miles of its 25 miles a cold-water creek. The creek is in the lower portion, rising from springs, flowing four miles, and then going underground. But the water has transformed the canyon, giving it new life, new dimensions, new perspectives.

There are no native fish in the creek, but both rainbow trout and long-eared sunfish have been introduced and they are thriving. The canyon, apart from the lower end, has never been grazed except by wild animals and so the grasses are luxuriant—tridents, gramas, bull muhly, and several dozen others. There are black walnuts, velvet ash, hop hornbeam, mulberry, mock orange, and desert willow along the creek and the huge faxon yucca, too. This species of yucca occurs nowhere else in any unit of our entire National Park System. Faxon yucca farther south reaches the height of 40 feet or more, but in McKittrick Canyon it rises to around 18 feet. Here is a rare pink rose (*R. woodsii*).

As one goes up the creek, he comes to big-tooth maple and several species of juniper and several species of oak. One of the oaks I saw is the chinquapin, common in the eastern United States. The madrone tree is here and also the southwestern chokecherry. The canyon has several kinds of fern, including the Arizona resurrection fern, and several dozens of kinds of grasses, including the blue-eyed grass (*Sisyrinchium*).

The bulblet fern that starts in Newfoundland has found its way to the South McKittrick Canyon. Solomon's seal has also arrived from the north and is to be found in humus along boulders in shade. A twining shrub, the bittersweet or waxwort, that reaches 20 feet or more in height is there, too. New to Texas is a valerian (*V. arizonica*); but this is found not in McKittrick Canyon proper

but high up about where the draw reaches the summit of the Guadalupes.

More than 20 species of insects new to science have been discovered in South McKittrick Canyon, a few representing brand-new genera. There is an abundance of uncommon species of reptiles. Scientific researchers expect manifold discoveries in many areas as the field work continues. To date, Dr. Frederick R. Gehlbach has identified more than 500 species of plants and shrubs; and the Park Service reports that in South McKittrick Canyon is "an association of plant species surviving today which represents a carry-over from the Pleistocene epoch of half a million years ago."

Some of the walls south of McKittrick Canyon are about 2,000 feet sheer. These limestone cliffs are treacherous, but with planning they could become, as Peter Koch observed, a fine place for a training station for young, prospective alpinists.

The hike up South McKittrick is one to take leisurely if the detail is to be absorbed. There are many contrasts. The north-facing slopes are thick with gray oak, juniper, and Texas madrone. The south-facing slopes are drier and here are the sotol, mimosa, and agave. The temperature on many of the south-facing slopes is apparently too high for tree growth since they receive more sunlight per unit than the north-facing slopes. Moreover, the sparser vegetation allows greater runoff from rainfall which carries away the ground litter, all of which makes for the perpetuation of a sparse countryside. The two sides, less than 500 yards apart, dramatize the relative effect of sunlight on vegetation.

Farther up the canyon are a few scattered ponderosa pine and a Douglas fir. Here also are blue quail (scaled quail) with a bushy white top and a few Mearn's quail with a soft, whinnying call. An occasional owl is heard. Hawks soar overhead. There is the happy song of the canyon wren; and swifts that nest high on the canyon walls dive on the traveler if he comes too close. A spring or summer visitor is bound to see a blue-gray gnatcatcher and a gray vireo, hunting insects.

The trail up South McKittrick Canyon goes about four and one half miles, the latter half of it being a rather rough road over or around big rocks, and at one point up through a three-sided chimney. It is untouched so far as man is concerned. I have only seen it in the winter and in the spring—never at a time when lightning is flashing and rain is falling. J. C. Hunter, Jr., has seen it when the rain came down in a deluge and lightning struck, filling the air with ozone and making the narrow canyon echo and re-echo for some minutes with the roar of thunder. Happily, lightning has never set a fire in the canyon, nor has man; so it remains in all of its pristine glory.

We sat in a natural limestone grotto outside the Hunter Lodge in South McKittrick eating dinner cooked over an open grill. Huge ponderosa pine shaded us. Our tables were made of heavy slab rock and we sat on rock benches. The talk was about South McKittrick and its future. The sentiment for making it a national park was rapidly growing; some land had already been acquired. The key unit was J. C. Hunter, Jr.'s 72,000-acre spread and he was eager to have it in the park. The naturalists had surveyed it and they, too, were eager. Stewart Udall, Secretary of the Interior, had preceded my first visit and he was enthusiastic.

We discussed the fact that there were parks and parks—of all kinds. Some state parks were merely amusement centers. In fact, most of the Texas parks are officially advertised as offering "dancing" as one of their attractions. The national parks have at times been so "developed" that their natural beauty has been ruined. Huge communities have sprung up in some, such as Yellowstone.

Noel Kincaid, who is not only a good ranch foreman and justice of the peace, but also the best architect of hot biscuits I ever knew, spoke up to say, "No road should ever git beyond this here Lodge."

Noel, I think, expressed the sentiments of all of us. The Lodge lies in the broad open mouth. Above it the canyon narrows and becomes a tortuous, winding passageway.

"A road would not only cost a fortune. It would ruin the place," Justice Jim Bowmer observed.

"This should be a place for hikers and walkers only," added Bob Burleson.

"Not only that," said Noel. "But those who walk the canyon should have a guide so that they get something out of it."

And that's about the size of it. South McKittrick Canyon is a relic forest or woodland going back to ancient days. It's a unique bit of America where history far beyond the period of man's appearance can be studied. History is being made each minute of the day and one with knowing eyes can see it and feel it with his fingers. I speak of the gummy lime being dissolved from the rock by the water of the creek, a soft layer deposited on rocks but not yet solidified. It does, however, harden fast, and as it hardens it makes a new channel for the water. Here is geological history being made.

"And don't forget to tell them about the piñon pine nuts, the best eating of all," said Noel.

"What about them?"

"Why, the rats of McKittrick collect them. Want a couple gallons? Okay, come with me and we'll find a rat's nest and rob it."

Peter Koch spoke up to talk about boys and girls yet unborn who could be educated in this canyon if it were left undisturbed.

"Had to rescue a couple of them trapped on a high cliff," said Noel.

"That will happen and it's one way of getting on terms with the outdoors," Peter replied. "But think of the opportunity to see a piece of the world as it was a million years ago."

South McKittrick Canyon is not the only repository of botanical wonders. Pine Canyon on the eastern slopes is another. It has no trail, and one who travels it goes on foot. But his rewards are as interesting as one who walks South McKittrick more leisurely.

North McKittrick Canyon is not without interest. It has a running stream in its upper reaches that stays above ground for a mile or so and then turns underground. Perhaps that is the reason that this canyon does not have the variety of plants that the other does.

North-bound travel on top of Capitan Reef is an exercise in mountaineering. This Reef is not a high plateau, but a vast expanse deeply eroded, filled with yawning canyons, steep cliffs, and precipitous slopes. A jeep road of sorts does run north from the Guadalupes into New Mexico. But it is a tortuous affair to negotiate, and those who dream of a tourist highway lined with camp sites coming down to Guadalupe Peak are having a pipe dream. Such a road could be designed, but it would be fantastically expensive. Moreover, all the camp sites would be "dry" camps as there is no water on top of Capitan Reef. Some who dream of these camps say that the water could be piped down from New Mexico. But there is a vast shortage of water in this contiguous New Mexico area. As one Forest Service official said, "To get water to the proposed high camps on the Guadalupes we'd have to take it down by helicopter."

There are a few ponds or springs in this desert land, and wherever one appears there usually is the vermilion flycatcher, the male according to the late Roy Bedichek being "a brilliant flaming gem," known to the Mexicans as *"brasita de fuego"* or "a little coal of fire." His scientific name, *Pyrocephalus,* indeed "signifies firehead" (*Adventures with a Texas Naturalist.* 1961 edition, p. 27). This bird has been moving north. "The vermilion flycatcher seems to love two physiographic features not often found in conjunction, viz., a desert, or semi-arid terrain, contiguous to a body of still water. This condition has been artificially created in many locations during recent years, especially in the Southwest." (p. 31). The vermilion flycatcher is now in the desert to the east of the Guadalupes and north of Bear Canyon at a place called Rattlesnake Springs. These springs are a detached section of Carlsbad Caverns National Park, and they have a pump house and permanent pond which provide the park headquarters with water. The vermilion flycatcher is now a year-round resident of Rattlesnake Springs.

The land adjacent to the Guadalupes on the north is the Lincoln National Forest in New Mexico, whose southern border is a part of North McKittrick Canyon. Lincoln National Forest (birthplace of famous Smokey Bear in the National Zoo, Washington, D.C.) lies between the Rio Grande and the Pecos, only its southern segment embracing Capitan Reef. Its northern reaches get into different geological formations, including 12,000-foot

Sierra Blanca with its popular ski lift, located in the Sacramento Mountains. In those northern parts are thick ponderosa stands and other conifers good for a Christmas-tree business. But Lincoln National Forest on the Capitan Reef has no commercial timber. Little islands of ponderosa pine can be found and a few Douglas fir, white fir, limber pine, and madrone. There are thick stands of a low oak shrub. But the trees are in an alligator juniper-piñon-pine complex, and have no value, except for fence posts. The grasses are mostly lush, the grama grasses and the muhly (or bull) grass being abundant. A low bush mountain mahogany is here and a ceonathus that I was not able to classify. But the familiar bear grass is present with plumes somewhat shorter than those in the Pacific Northwest.

Chukor were planted near Sitting Bull Falls and they are doing well. Dove and quail frequent the valleys. Wild turkey seem to be holding their own. Mule deer are plentiful. A herd of elk north of North McKittrick Canyon has mixed with the herd on the main Guadalupes in Texas and they have a peculiar migration habit. They move north in the spring to the lower elevations of Capitan Reef and south, to higher land, in the winter. " 'Tain't natural," one New Mexican rancher told me. "But the reason is probably that they follow the bloom of the sotol, of which they are very fond."

We sat on the northern rim of North McKittrick Canyon having lunch—R. E. Rea, supervisor of this forest, Paul Webb, superintendent of the nearby Carlsbad Caverns National Park, and I. It was a clear January day; and while a cold, biting northwest wind had whipped us all morning as we came by jeep down the rim of the western escarpment of Capitan Reef, we were now drenched in warm sunshine.

North McKittrick dropped so precipitously that someone remarked it would be slow work to go horseback into its yawning pit. The broken land at its head also shows very steep slopes

and sharp cliffs, making travel on horseback difficult. While Capitan Reef is one entity, the deep folds between the Guadalupes
and the Lincoln Forest indicate that lines of communication
should be graded trails for foot or horse travel, not highways.

This southern portion of the Lincoln Forest that abuts the
North McKittrick Canyon (and includes a part of it) adjoins
Carlsbad Caverns National Park to the northeast. Carlsbad and
the Guadalupes should be either one integrated park or two
parks under close management. In either event a corridor of
land should be taken from the Lincoln Forest and used to unite
the two. There has never been much Forest Service use of this
corridor, only a couple of grazing permits. The Forest Service
has ambitious plans, actively under way, to build a crescent-
shaped highway into this area so as to develop auto camp sites.
Many of them would be "dry" camps, as there is little water on
the ridges. Others would be located at falls or near springs in
the canyons. A network of foot trails would lace the area. This
development would open up a magnificent segment of Capitan
Reef to recreation.

But if the corridor were under park management, a continuous road system with camp sites and a trail system stretching from
Carlsbad Caverns to El Capitan could be developed. Carlsbad
Caverns is so heavily saturated with tourists that some dispersion
of them is needed.

There is talk of putting a chair lift up Bear Canyon to the
Bowl and creating there a motel and restaurant center out of
which hiking groups could operate and eventually find their
way to Carlsbad Caverns. Whatever plan ultimately is adopted,
Carlsbad Caverns and the Guadalupes need to be closely integrated in management.

That's about the way the issue stands as respects this part of
the wilderness of Texas. Great values ride on the decisions yet
to be made.

Now that a new national park has been created in the Guadalupes, will the new caretakers recognize how fragile this desert-mountain country is and guard against "development"? This is not a wholly theoretical question, for, as the years go by, the National Park Service seems to be getting further and further away from the historical concept of a national park.

The purpose of a national park as defined by Congress (39 Stat. 535) is "to conserve the scenery and the natural and historic objects and the wildlife therein and to provide for the enjoyment of the same in such manner and by such means as will leave them unimpaired for the enjoyment of future generations."

This language, read in the ordinary sense, would indicate that the wildness inherent in a park should remain inviolate. The National Park Service has different ideas. Rather than keep a park's wildness inviolate by putting civilization on the perimeter, it penetrates the sanctuary with roads, campgrounds, hotels, houses, and other developments. Some parks have veritable "cities" within their borders. Not many are "developed" by bringing civilization only to the edges. The tendency of the Park Service is, indeed, to penetrate deeper and deeper into these sanctuaries with "development" programs.

Peter Farb, conservationist and naturalist, writing in *The Christian Science Monitor* for October 17, 1966, stated that our national parks are "in deep trouble," that the National Park Service is so maladministered that the question is not whether national parks will be left "unimpaired" for future generations, but whether they can be kept "unimpaired for even this generation."

Seven thousand boats have destroyed the quiet beauty of Yellowstone Lake and practically driven all wildlife from it. The roads of Yellowstone are clogged by cars that run bumper to bumper. Stands of trees are more and more cut to construct trailer camps and parking lots. One new "development" in Yellowstone is a supermarket, trinket shop, laundry and "over 1000 gimcrack cabins." A recently built parking lot helped destroy Daisy Geyser. The wolf is gone. The coyote, protected by the Department of the Interior and the Park Service in the summer, is destroyed in the winter on bounties given by the same Department.

The destruction of predators has led to a disastrous increase in elk. They have indeed multiplied so fast they have destroyed their habitat and they in turn have to be slaughtered by the thousands.

What has happened in Yellowstone has happened in other national parks. All have been so opened to motorized travel that traffic jams have mounted and wildlife has fled. The mass invasion into Rocky Mountain National Park caused acres of unique tundra vegetation to be trampled out of existence. While the Department of the Interior with one hand purports to preserve wilderness, with the other it promotes destruction. Its Bureau of Reclamation is the agency responsible for the great threat to Grand Canyon, which many think is our noblest scene.

Congress in the Wilderness Act of 1964 (78 Stat. 890) defined "wilderness" anew and gave the National Park Service a new mandate. Congress provided:

> A wilderness, in contrast with those areas where man and his own works dominate the landscape, is hereby recognized as an area where the earth and its community of life are untrammeled by man, where man himself is a visitor who does not remain. An area of wilderness is further defined to mean in this Act an area of undeveloped Federal land retaining its primeval character and influence, without permanent improvements or human habitation, which is protected and managed so as to preserve its natural conditions and which (1) generally appears to have been affected primarily by the forces of nature,

with the imprint of man's work substantially unnoticeable; (2) has outstanding opportunities for solitude or a primitive and unconfined type of recreation; (3) has at least five thousand acres of land or is of sufficient size as to make practicable its preservation and use in an unimpaired condition; and (4) may also contain ecological, geological, or other features of scientific, educational, scenic, or historical value.

Congress directed the Secretary of the Interior within ten years to review "every roadless area of five thousand contiguous acres or more" and to report to the President its suitability "for preservation as wilderness."

It is discouraging and alarming to view the manner in which the Park Service has approached this undertaking.

As this is written, the Park Service is willing to preserve only 47 per cent of the 512,674 acres in the Great Smoky Mountains National Park as wilderness. It has ambitious plans to "develop" the rest, including highways.

As this is written, the Park Service is seeking to preserve only 49,800 acres of the 106,934 acres in the Lassen Volcanic National Park.

As this is written, the Park Service is promoting a North Cascades National Park which would include Pickett Range— probably the wildest, most pristine stretch of wilderness that we have outside of Alaska. It plans to "develop" the Pickett Range so that tourists can pour into it by motorized equipment.

As this is written, the Park Service has ambitious plans for using funiculars inside wilderness areas of national parks to transport in an effortless way hordes of people into those sanctuaries.

The National Park Service, in other words, has become not a conservator of wilderness and its values, but a promoter of "development." Conservationists are, therefore, likely to be shocked when they realize that their struggle to get a national park in the Guadalupes was a Pyrrhic victory, that while they had expected preservation of a wilderness, their inheritance was a "development" program.

"Parks for people" is the new slogan of the National Park Service. It is the chief promoter of overuse that will most certainly see the few remaining vignettes of wild America destroyed in only a few decades.

These were my thoughts as I left the Guadalupes the last time. Those mountains do not have the recuperative power of those in New England or in the Pacific West. They are dry and fragile. Overuse would come very quickly here in West Texas. For the Guadalupes to survive this generation and remain "unimpaired" for future generations, they must be treated tenderly and discreetly. They must be idolized for their rarity and uniqueness—not converted into a Coney Island. Their sacred precincts should be invaded only by those who can go on foot or muleback. Their oasis high above the Chihuahua Desert should be reserved for the adventurous. Those who find their pleasure in dancing and drinking beer can be entertained along the skirts of these great mountains.

The Ahabs of which I speak are not all in private industry or in local government. Some are firmly entrenched in seats in Washington, D.C. As a result, the Guadalupes may yet be the victims of official vandalism. For man, whether he wears a Federal uniform or works for a lumber company or a mining company or is in the livestock business, can be even more destructive than goats. And it is the goats that have wasted much of Texas and laid bare most of the Middle East and North Africa.

CHAPTER XI

THE HILL COUNTRY

I had visited Edwards Plateau many times but had never seen it with knowing eyes. My trips were to places such as Austin for dinners or lectures or to San Antonio for social or professional engagements. These towns are on the edge of the Plateau. But I had never looked closely at its geological, botanical, and historical anatomy.

It is predominantly limestone from 600 feet to 800 feet thick and it is a large area perhaps 200 miles east and west and 100 miles north and south and tips from west to east. It lies west and north of an escarpment that starts near San Antonio, runs north into Blanco and Llano counties, then west along the top of Kimble, dropping to include the southern parts of Sutten and Crockett, then south to the Gulf west of the Pecos River. East and south of this line are the prairies; west and north of it is the Hill Country. It's not high, never reaching more than 2,800 feet above sea level. The fault that borders the Hill Country on the south and east is called Balcone, that being Spanish for balcony, and this escarpment does at points have the appearance of perpendicular galleries capped by balconies.

The geology of the area, is, however, much more complex than I have suggested. Above the escarpment are other faults almost without number—faults that produce hillocks, hills, and ridges, often extending dozens of miles. A ridge may have worn away, leaving a mesa that stands in isolation. Deep ravines may present a jungle of boulders and brush too difficult for a man on horseback. In other areas a river has left an alluvial plain a half-mile or so wide where cotton was once grown and now the small cereals. In still others a river fed by springs offers banks where hiking trails could be built. West of Kerrville the Plateau flattens out for some miles and is fairly level at a 2,000-foot elevation. Which of these conditions is typical of the Plateau is difficult to say. The more I traveled it, the more diverse it seemed to become. If there is a typical piece of the Plateau it probably is in a wild tangle of ravines and bluffs where cedar (the local name for juniper) and oak grow in profusion.

The Spanish established a trail known as El Camino Real (the King's Highway) that started in Mexico, came through San Antonio and Austin, crossed the Sabine River at Pendleton's Ferry and on to Natchitoches, Louisiana, and east to Natchez, Mississippi. This trail crossed 12 rivers, including the Rio Grande. The key to its use were fords providing passage for heavily laden pack trains and Mexican carts. It was along this route that the Franciscan Fathers plodded to establish missions in the Hill Country. By the 1820s the first North American settlers were arriving there. They settled first on the edges of the Hill Country, the Indians making its caves, springs, and ravines their refuge.

This is now a friendly land where milk means buttermilk; potatoes, sweet ones; peas, the black-eyed variety; sweet bread, cake; tea, iced tea; light bread, loaf bread; blinky, sour milk; batter cakes, hot cakes; goobers, peanuts.

The first settlers built stone fences as the New Englanders did; and remnants of them are still visible. But when barbed wire came in the 1870s and 1880s, it gradually displaced them at a cost of about $1,200 a mile or even more.

The Plateau is well supplied with water. The rainfall is about 28 or 30 inches a year. Prior to the Agricultural Adjustment Act, the runoffs were sometimes severe, flash floods roaring down slick limestone river beds and ripping up huge, stately pecan trees. With the AAA came water impoundments that ranchers call "tanks." They often hold water for months on end, saving the soil and providing water for cattle, sheep, and goats. A small plane flight shows dozens of these "tanks," many of which have water for only a few months. But others are permanent deep-water tanks fed by springs as well as by rain water. AAA now promotes conversion of these "tanks" into fish ponds, following the example of Israel. Many now produce large-mouth bass, cat-fish, and brim, some of the best producers being on the LBJ ranches in Blanco County.

President Johnson spoke of this Hill Country in his 1965 State of the Union Message:

"It was once barren land. The angular hills were covered with scrub cedar and a few live oaks. Little would grow in the harsh caliche soil. And each spring the Pedernales River would flood the valley.

"But men came and worked and endured and built.

"Today that country is abundant with fruit, cattle, goats, and sheep. There are pleasant homes, and lakes, and the floods are gone."

Limestone is porous and cavernous and usually a generous purveyor of water. When I think of the Hill Country, I think of limestone, though many other types of rocks and sands are also present. I picture it as beginning with a rim (noticeable even to one who travels by car) that dips west of Belton in Bell County. Technically, this is north of the Edwards Plateau. But it was near here that I visited my first limestone cave. We ate at the Stage Coach Inn that took care of the needs of travelers when the old Chisholm Trail flourished. It was named for a mixed-blood Cherokee, Jesse Chisholm, and ran from San Antonio north to Oklahoma and across that state to Abilene, Texas. I went down wooden stairs 30 feet or more into a cavern as large as my garage at home and stood in adoration of a clear, deep, pure-water spring that had been running from time out of mind. Limestone caves are everywhere on the Edwards Plateau. To-day one commonly pumps well water. In the old days one drilled a hundred feet or more to get a flowing well. At other times the water fairly spouted from the ground in small cascades. Such indeed are the headwaters of the Frio River in Real County. Prade Ranch, which is a post office and once was a fine dude ranch, lies at the head of the Frio and a trip out of it on foot or by jeep shows how a river is made. One source is a quiet pool lined with ferns and mosses as thick as any that Maine can produce. Most of the springs are small spouts and they all join to form a stream whose bottom for a couple of miles is a flat sheet of limestone. It is so flat and smooth as to make an ideal roadbed. Jeeps negotiate it to this day, and one can see in the limestone the rutted tracks of old wagons of the Conestoga type coming from San Angelo or Abilene headed east toward Kerrville. The problem was to reach the relatively flat top of Edwards Plateau; and the Frio River offered the passageway with a steep climb.

The Edwards Plateau is often called the Land of 1,100 Springs. How many there are is not known. Lampasas is marked by springs that start a river by that name. The waters are in part medicinal and the town was once a thriving spa.

San Antonio Park has many springs both on San Pedro Creek and on the San Antonio, and the city has exploited them in the cause of recreation, civic beauty, and water supply.

The city of San Antonio that sits on the Edwards Plateau is entirely supplied by wells from these underlying limestone deposits. There are a number of rivers in the San Antonio area. The San Antonio River runs out of the Plateau and does not contribute to it. This river is sometimes called the Holy Spring of Father Margil. Don Antonio Margil de Jesus was active in Texas during the first quarter of the eighteenth century. One of his trips to the Hill Country was described by E. G. Littlejohn in *Texas Folk-Lore Society:*

> Father Margil was with a company of priests and soldiers spying out the land when they were almost overcome by the heat and drought. At length they came into a valley where there was green grass for the horses but not a drop of water. The priests kneeled under a tree to pray for water, and as he prayed Father Margil's eye fell on bunches of mustang grapes above him. With praises to God, he began to climb for the juicy fruit. While he was reaching for a cluster, he fell. In falling, he swung to the grapevine and somehow uprooted it with a sudden jerk. Then from the hole left by the root a plenteous and refreshing spring of water gushed out. Thus was the origin of what is now called the San Antonio River.

Comal Springs near New Braunfels is one of the prettiest and most affluent, its clear water being adorned by the pennywort with an umbrella-shaped leaf that grows under the water, and its sides being lined with the *anacua* tree whose leaves are rough like a hound's tongue. Comal Springs feeds a huge swimming pool several hundred yards long. The flow out of Comal Springs produces rapids that people shoot, lying flat on inflated rubber tubes to a point on the swelling river where one can get to the shore.

Los Moras Springs near Bracketville flow more than 14 million gallons a day and feed the Los Moras River.

San Marcos Springs heads up the San Marcos River and forms big pools where glass-bottomed boats are run; and to keep the underwater view intact, the proprietors of the project weed the bottom. About 100 million gallons of water a day flow out of springs into the San Marcos.

Barton Springs, near Austin, is the fifth largest in Texas and flows about 27 million gallons a day; with a whole series of smaller springs it feeds Barton Creek and the Colorado River. Like most of the large springs in the Hill Country, Barton Springs is neatly groomed and manicured. It is indeed a part of the Austin park system. The water has a 70° F. temperature the year round. It's an ideal swimming hole that many enjoy. Jim Hart—Austin lawyer in his eighties—swims in it every day. "I figure that's why Jim Hart's so hard to beat in any jury case," Byron Lockhart of the Austin bar told me. Byron Lockhart, whose forebears came from the Big Thicket, was with us on several of these Texas explorations. Whether he is a reliable reporter became much mooted on account of the tales he told. For it was on one of my trips into the Hill Country, which as we shall see is thick with cattle, that he spoke to Justice Jim Bowmer about my hat that has been with me on hundreds of trips: "If I saw it in a cow pasture, I'd step over it!"

Del Rio, far to the south of Austin, has the San Felipe Springs that flow 65 million gallons a day. The main springs rise in a limestone pocket from which four pumps carry much of the water to the city's municipal water system. These springs never went down in the seven-year drought of the 1950s but in 1964 their flow dropped one-third and the people were worried. The springs, however, came back. I walked with W. C. Hodge of Del Rio through the manicured grounds where these springs rise and talked with him about the early settlers who naturally made their settlements near them. Finally I asked him if anyone knew about the source of the water bubbling out of this limestone. He said that some of the smaller springs of San Felipe reflected surface drainage, as their water became discolored when it rained hard. "But the big San Felipe Springs are as clear as crystal no matter how hard the rain."

Our talk turned to the underground reservoirs that feed these springs. "Some say that San Felipe water comes from the Rocky Mountains. But I don't think so."

"What is your view?"

"Well, I'll tell you. Some years back a rancher pulled out of Del Rio in a wagon drawn by two mules. He got as far as Kerrville and got messing around one of the big springs up there when his whole outfit fell in."

After a long pause he added, "Never did find the rancher but the two mules and the wagon came out here at San Felipe."

I have mentioned so far the springs of the Hill Country that have been made into parks or that have been developed as recreational centers by private enterprise. But there are others that are still in the rough and that need preservation and protection as parks or as recreational units owned by such conservation groups as Nature Conservancy.

Hamilton Pool near Cedar Valley and about thirty-two miles from Austin is one. Limestone has dissolved, forming a huge sinkhole and the rim above is cirque-like forming a crescent several hundred feet long and 50 feet or more above the bottom of the hole. Basin Creek pours over the rim at several places to form what Congressman W. R. Poage has called "the most beautiful three acres in Texas." The overhang of the rim is in places about 100 feet wide and under it ferns are abundant. The pool and the river, running to the Pedernales, are filled with bass. The stream passes through a stand of giant cypress and nourishes pasture land now overgrazed by cattle and by sheep. Hamilton Pool, privately owned, needs saving. It is a sanctuary dominated by the soothing sound of falling water. Man needs this place of solitude as a refuge.

Not far from Kendalia is Edge Falls. It, too, has a rim high above a solution hole, a rim with an overhang of 50 to 100 feet. One huge spout of water roars off the rim; but at the base of the cliffs other springs also bubble forth. The creek does not go far before it runs over lesser cascades for 100 yards or so, making a unique picture, seen from below. Cypress trees heavy with Spanish moss line the small watercourse. One cypress is at least 10 feet in diameter. This creek that never runs dry feeds the Guadalupe River. Edge Falls is popular with sight-seers, the owner making a fair living out of entrance fees alone. But the threat of goat grazing is always present, a prospect that upsets the botanists. For as Donovan S. Correll says, "It would be stupid to put goats in the Edge Falls Canyon. For that canyon has the extremely rare and almost extinct small tree, *Styrax platanifolia*, the sycamore-leaf storax."

Pausing a moment, he added, "It is the only place that I have seen it in Texas."

The 700 Springs below Telegraph, Texas, on Route 377, would be harder to preserve, for they cover a rather long stretch of the Llano River where eight-pound bass and 20-pound catfish are caught. They pour out of low limestone cliffs along the river and about eight feet or 10 feet above it. Before the drought of the 1950s they were much higher on the cliffs. But they never came back to that level, the floor of the pool from which they came apparently having dropped. But this stretch of the Llano, now used as grazing land for cattle, sheep, and goats, must in time be either in the public domain or under private recreational auspices. For the Llano and its 700 Springs are one of the wonders of this world.

Jacob's Well, reached through a field thick with prickly poppies (white, red, and lavender), heads up Cypress Creek which in turn feeds the Blanco River. Located about two miles west of Wimberley, it flows 1,000 gallons a minute. It seems as if it has hardly been discovered it is so far off the beaten path. In nestles under 12-foot granite cliffs ideal for a high dive and is as clear, pure, and cold as any in Maine.

Jacob's Well is in country where wild turkeys, deer, and

armadillos live; and one who crosses the fields and enters the woods is apt to see one or all of them. Jacob's Well has a Biblical significance to stockmen in the Hill Country, for in years of drought it has always been a sure source of water. It is said to be 2,300 feet deep, widening, as one drops, from a well eight feet in diameter for the first 100 feet to one that is 100 feet wide. It is in this well that two young skin divers were trapped and drowned in 1964.

The rivers of the Edwards Plateau have been extensively dammed, mainly for flood control and for hydroelectric power. Most of these dams, such as Buchanan Dam on the Colorado, produce reservoirs with highly fluctuating water levels that greatly detract from recreational use. The Alvin Wirtz Dam below the conjunction of the Colorado and Llano has produced Lyndon B. Johnson Lake whose water level fluctuates but little. This 25-mile expanse of clear, cold water is already a favorite recreational spot on the Plateau; it is used in the winter by fishermen; it is heavily used in the summer for swimming, boating, water-skiing—by President Johnson and a host of others. Its shore lines are fast developing as attractive residential sites. Of the people that use and enjoy it, probably two-thirds live there year round now, mostly in retirement.

The Edwards Plateau is nourished by eight rivers—the West Nueces, Nueces, Frio, Dry Frio, Hondo Creek, Medina, Guadalupe, and Sabinal. Waters of these rivers are diverted for irrigation and for other local uses. But the main reliance for municipal supply is on the aquifers within the limestone. Experience shows that most of these aquifers are renewable.

Some aquifers are nonrenewable pools which when sucked dry remain dry so far as man can predict. Big Spring, Texas, sucked its spring dry sometime during the 1920s; and dry it now is. Comanche Springs at Fort Stockton that in recent times produced 30 million gallons a day is now apparently dry for all time. About twenty miles east of Fort Stockton is Tunis Spring, one of the old chain of springs that marked the route of the stagecoaches across Texas. One searches in vain for the glitter, the gleam, or the smell of water anywhere. Comal Springs at New Braunfels that flowed 220 million gallons a day went dry during the severe drought of the 1950s but now flows again.

The Edwards Plateau underground reservoir is about 175 miles long and from three to 30 miles wide, and it extends under several counties, including Uvalde, Medina, Bexar, Comal, and Hays.

The recharge area of the reservoir (or the area where this ground-water bearing formation comes to the surface) is a strip (Balcones fault zone) of faulted and porous limestone where water goes underground into the reservoir. Southward-flowing streams that cross the Balcones fault zone lose a large part of their water to the underground reservoir, and rain falling directly on this faulted zone also adds to the recharge. The streams that contribute most of the water drain that area of the Edwards Plateau below a line generally from the city of Rocksprings to the city of Blanco.

Annual flow of water into the reservoir was as little as 44,000 acre-feet in 1956, and as much as 1,700,000 acre-feet in 1958. The annual average recharge from 1934 to 1959 was about 500,000 acre-feet. Usage from the reservoir in 1963 was 277,000 acre-feet. (An acre-foot of water is the amount which will cover an area of one acre one foot deep or about 326,000 gallons.)

Water is pumped out by hundreds of wells from Brackettville to Kyle. The reservoir is the only source of water for the cities of Uvalde, Knippa, Sabinal, D'Hanis, Hondo, Castroville, LaCoste, San Antonio, New Braunfels, San Marcos, Kyle, and other smaller communities. Irrigation, industrial, domestic, stock, and other uses also are dependent on water from the reservoir.

To repeat, while the water table in parts of the Edwards

Plateau has been falling, most of it is renewable. Yet worry and concern have made water conservation a prime legislative objective.

All of Central Texas and all of West Texas are worried about water. Midland, Texas, in 1965 paid $750,000 for a 20,200-acre West Texas ranch that has enough underground water, it is said, to supply the city's needs for almost a century. The city of Amarillo has also purchased the water rights under a large tract of land for more than 1 million dollars. Some areas have aquifers which are renewable. Others draw their water from aquifers that are seemingly nonrenewable pools of water that have accumulated over eons of time. The geologists say that the city of Lubbock is one of the latter. It has grown into a tremendous farming center by reason of irrigation from underground water. Now that the water supply is playing out, some people in Lubbock are getting panicky. The pressure is on to transport water long distances to this area, an area which many think should not in the first place have been developed so extensively for that type of farming.

Texas law provides for the creation of underground water conservation districts and one, the Edwards Underground Water District, has been formed, embracing the counties of Uvalde, Medina, Bexar, Comal, and Hays. This district regulates drilling for water and the spacing of wells; it seeks to remedy waste; and it makes plans for conservation of water and replenishment of the aquifers, where percolating waters are found.

Its geologists have learned where the faults which characterize the Plateau provide seepage of rain water into the aquifers. By measuring stream flow they know that some water from some rivers works its way through those faults into the aquifers. Now plans are afoot to build dams at strategic points not for flood control, not for hydroelectric power, not for irrigation, but for renewal of the aquifers. The idea is to locate a dam above the points in a river bed where the main seepage points lie and then to release the water in dry periods in small amounts that will feed aquifers through these seepage fractures.

Studies show that a system of reservoirs above the recharge areas on the streams west of Bexar County can increase the average annual recharge by a total of about 100,000 acre-feet. It is estimated that by like measures the average annual recharge on the Nueces, Frio, and Sabinal rivers can be increased by a total of 68,200 acre-feet per year. Thus geological knowledge will transform parts of the Edwards Plateau in the interests of a permanent water system—if modern Ahabs I will mention can be controlled.

Edwards Plateau, with elevations from 700 feet to 2,800 feet, reaches its highest point near Rocksprings in Edwards County (for whom the Plateau is named). Streams radiate in all directions from this point. They give Texas the cool, scenic Hill Country— one of the finest, unexploited, recreational areas in the country, ranking right along with West Virginia, Vermont, and western Massachusetts and Connecticut. I went to the Hill Country thinking of Texas as a dry, sunburned land. I discovered cool river bottoms in the deep shade of elegant pecan trees.

Hunting pecans is a Texas experience, as F. W. van Emden writes in *Sure Enough, How Come?* (1938):

> Let's go and hunt the wild and dangerous Pecan!
> Let's track him to his den,
> In bottoms deep,
> On hillsides steep,
> And many a rocky glen.
> A branch might fall and hit your head,
> A limb may break and you'll be dead.
> Rivals a tree may flay,
> Nuts hit your dome,
> A heavy rock might stray,

They'd carry you home.
You might slip and muddy shores are sleek.
And if you trip, how icy are the waters of the creek.
If it's the grass you're searching in
And soles upon your shoes are thin,
Pecans are bound to bruise,
Just like a stone, your skin.
Thorns may scratch
Poison oak shoots may be near
Who hunts pecans must overcome his fear.
Search under fallen leaves,
Where many snakes abide,
Anti-crotalus serum,
They'll sure shoot in your hide.
Pecans are tiger-striped and tawny,
How crafty is their tumbling flight!
So since it takes a hunter brawny,
I think to hunt pecans is right.

There is ever clear, sparkling water near these pecan stands—with springs or singing brooks. And higher up are lush meadows brilliant with bluebonnets.

The bluebonnet of the Hill Country is *L. texensis*, not *L. subcarnosus*, the official Texas species. But few know the difference; and one is as showy as the other.

Slopes are ablaze with the golden-mane (*Coreopsis basalis*), and rights of way along the main roads are brilliant with the Indian blanket-flower (*Gaillardia pulchella*).

Edwards Plateau has a botany similar to that of Mexico, according to Donovan S. Correll, the noted botanist. "It is curiously as closely related to Mexico as are the Chisos Mountains which lie next to Mexico," he said.

Every April the soapberry tree (*Sapindus Drummondii*) blooms and the fragrance of the bee bush fills the air.

The Hill Country has unique botanical wonders. The rare

American smoke tree (*Continus americanus*) is found on the Blanco River.

The rare endemic, sycamore-leaf silverbell tree (*Styrax platanifolia*), with white bell-shaped flowers, is found in ravines below Edge Falls, just south of Kendalia in Kendall County.

There, too, is found the red-flowered American columbine—those ravines being one of its last refuges in Texas.

The wild barberry (*Berberis Swaseyi*) is an uncommon endemic to the Edwards Plateau.

The mustang grape with its light-colored underleaf that sparkles in a light breeze covers many trees. It makes a delicious wine and the late J. Frank Dobie had a recipe for it:

> Draw off the juice into a clean vessel, and dissolve in it from two to three pounds of sugar to the gallon, but be sure to put no water in, and no liquor. Put it away in a barrel or other suitable vessel to ferment, with a small venthole left open; watch it until the fermentation ceases, which can be told by the cessation of the noise of simmering. Then cork it up tight, and keep twelve months, and it will begin to have a body and be considered good wine.
>
> But none should ever be used before it is a year old, and after that the older it is, the better.—John C. Duval, *First Texas Man of Letters* (1939) p. 60.

Dr. Correll found near Spanish Pass the *Onosmodium Helleri* or Heller's marbleseed. "It is one of the rarest plants that we have in Texas," he told me. "It grows about a foot tall and its stem has large round leaves about five inches in diameter which are as rough as a hound's tongue, in fact, it belongs to what is often called the 'Hound's Tongue' family. It has a rather inconspicuous flower and very hard marbly seeds. It was named for Dr. A. A. Heller, one of the botanical collectors in Texas who originally found it. This plant belongs to the same family in which *Lithosperum ruderale* is found. This latter plant was used by the southwestern Indians in abortion or for birth control. The English made a study of it and it is the source, or rather the result, of our modern-day birth-control pills."

Two species of buckeye—one with large clusters of scarlet flowers and the other with cream-colored flowers—are scattered over this region.

Two evergreens—the Texas persimmon whose trunk resembles the crepe myrtle and the Texas mountain laurel which has massive clusters of royal purple flowers—mark the Hill Country.

There also are two varieties of redbud whose flowers are rose-colored and thus somewhat different from the cerise redbud of the Potomac Valley.

In the spring, winecups, Indian paintbrushes, bluebonnets, malvas, sphaeralceas, several species of gaillardias, and many others give a flourish of color to the landscape. Many species flower right on through from March to October, while some have two periods of flowering—spring and fall. Many species in the sunflower family, such as black-eyed Susans, thelesperma, helianthus, berlandiera and lindheimera, the Texas-star, as well as species in the gentian, phlox, dogwood, bean, and other families are unusually ornamental.

Many botanists have explored the Hill Country, one of the foremost being Ferdinand Jacob Lindheimer whose field work was done between 1843 and 1852; and his collections are still treasured by Harvard University and the Missouri Botanical Garden.

Come spring the woodpeckers and flycatchers move in. The black-chinned hummingbird is busy. Bass rise to a fly, making a swirl that startles.

The blooms pass and summer settles down. The limestone waters refresh the swimmers. The deep shade of pecans and cypress along the watercourses is inviting. Sailboats, motorboats, and canoes multiply on the watercourses.

There are elms on the Plateau and some are as stately as any I have seen in New England. One at President Johnson's birthplace near Johnson City makes shade that is 100 feet across.

Fall brings bright colors. The wild cherries that gave a touch of white in May are now crimson.

There are some sugar maples on the Plateau and fall gives them the brilliant colors of New England.

Sumac heavy with berries is red. Leaves of the Spanish oak have a touch of gold. The Hill Country has a small evergreen tree called yaupon (*Ilex vomitoria*) whose leaves are leathery like American holly and whose berries are a deep port red when the frosts arrive. The burr oak and red oak add splashes of red. But the most spectacular fall tree of all is the wild china (*Sapindus Drummondii*) whose oblong leaves and large pea-sized fruit turn golden to make a startling plume in a green-brown forest.

Limestone, while porous and an ideal conduit of water, does not produce prime soils. At least the limestone soils in the Hill Country are not so rich as its granite soils. In the LBJ ranch country the saying is that the soils north of the Pedernales are better than those south of it. The reason is that granite lies to the north.

This granite boiled up eons ago and today appears as low weathered knobs, polished by wind and rain. The limestone came later when the ocean invaded and lay over the land for centuries on end. The marine life made the limestone; the fossils are so numerous they are beyond counting. While the limestone covered the granite in many places, islands of it stood high above the sea, and those are landmarks today. Marble Falls in Llano County (just north of the LBJ ranch) is one. A lively granite quarry business is located there; it cuts and polishes granite for facings or for building blocks. It produced the granite used to build the capital building in Austin. Its debris makes excellent jetty rock for sea walls.

West of Marble Falls, and also in Llano County, is the Enchanted Rock at whose feet Sandy Creek runs.

Mesquite, oak, and hickory provide much shade along the Sandy. Here, too, are spreading elms and the red buckeye (*Aesculus pavia*).

Some cardinals and a talkative mockingbird greeted us. A road runner sped up Sandy Creek and chipping sparrows were higher on the rock. Enchanted Rock has an exposed dome that is 640 acres in size. The south side has an easy incline, while the north is a steep cliff. Other granite peaks join the Rock to form a long, low pre-Cambrian ridge.

The Enchanted Rock collects water in pockets and around these pockets interesting water plants grow, including a wide range of ferns. Lichens first take hold of the polished rock. Over the centuries they accumulate debris which in turn produces mosses. The ferns follow in that sequence.

The Rock, that is a landmark on the old Pinta Trail that Indians used traveling north and south, was held in awe by them. It apparently made noises—a phenomenon caused by the expansion and contraction of the granite as it cooled after a hot day. It also made noises when people walked on the crust that lies over it. Its mica glistened in the sun, producing "spirit fires." It was indeed a holy place for the Indians, and much early history of the white man's attempt to settle and survey this Hill Country is written around the Enchanted Rock. Last century the Reverend Mr. Dan More held services on top of it, members of his church riding horses or hiking to the top to hear his sermon based on Matt. 16:18: "Upon this rock I will build my church."

South of the Enchanted Rock in Gillespie County is the Balanced Rock. This, too, is granite country and one hikes over and around huge boulders and through scrub oak and the bee bush (*Aloysia lycioides*), that ranchers despise, to a low ridge. The Rock is neatly balanced on two small points; and it is seemingly so delicately poised that it invites a push. Many have tried and none has succeeded. A red-faced, bald-headed man out of breath after the short climb told me, "Looks to me as if a man could do it if he had a wife he'ping him, worth her salt."

I have seen the tumbled granite boulders leading up to the Balanced Rock in a yellow sea of coreopsis. Here I found a cucumber (*Tillandsia recurvata*) where ball moss grows on the oak trees. As I neared the top a scarlet tanager flew by and a canyon wren started singing "The sweetest song in Texas."

These are not the only granite glories of the Edwards Plateau. But they illustrate its diversity. Ranchmen love granite, for it produces the most nutritious soils.

"Don't have to use store feed on cattle if they're fed on Llano County granite," one big-framed rancher told me.

"Flowers also thicker and brighter," Don Correll added.

Yet limestone has wonders and glories of its own.

North of the Edwards Plateau—but in older limestone country —is Glen Rose, county seat of Somervell County, the smallest in Texas.

Glen Rose was on the old Comanche Trail and the first settlers were exposed to many raids. A fort was built and its remnants are still visible. It was settled in 1840 and planted to cotton, slave labor being used.

Glen Rose scuttlebutt is that John Wilkes Booth, assassinator of Lincoln, escaped and lived for years at Glen Rose, running a bar. People will even show you the house where he is said to have lived.

An old-timer gave me a poem commemorating this pleasant place:

> Locked within the rock-ribbed hills
>   Where flow a thousand rippling rills,
> And with the circling Cedars crowned
>   Where vales, like facial smiles abound,
> Like glory of a sunset's close,
>   A Gem, a Jewel called Glen Rose.

In front of the courthouse on the city square is a dinosaur track picked out of the rocky limestone bed of the Paluxy River and imbedded in a wall for display purposes. Its mineral water—once supporting a well-known spa—still bubbles from a fountain and as I drank, an old-timer hollered "Good for what may be ailin' your kidneys or stomach."

Nearby is a sign that reads in part:

> The best way to see the famous prehistoric dinosaur tracks is [to] contact a representative of the Somervell County Historical Society in the courthouse and arrange for a guided tour.
>
> If you want to hike it or drive it alone you should study this map. Stop for small tours at "Tourist Information" signs. You are warned not to go on private property without permission. It is a violation of the law to excavate, disturb, deface, disfigure, damage, destroy, or remove any fossilized foot print . . .

The big map shows the course of the Paluxy River and the location of some of the dinosaur tracks—an area which Congressman W. R. Poage of Texas, by a bill introduced on June 21, 1966, seeks to have made into the Dinosaur Trail National Monument.

Mr. Eugene G. Connally showed me the dinosaur tracks in the river bed, all as described by the *National Geographic* in its May, 1954, issue. On the way we stopped to see Shaky Springs where the earth trembles when one jumps up and down, there probably being a relatively thin crust of earth over a subterranean limestone pool.

Shaky Springs is near the Paluxy River west of Glen Rose and is owned by Lester Trimble who raises Shetland ponies. Shaky Springs is his reserve water supply. One friend told Mr. Trimble that Shaky Springs was an underground lake "which has turned over." How deep it is, no one knows. Mr. Trimble has probed for the bottom with 50-foot rods and has not reached it.

The Paluxy River has worn away the limestone, uncovering

the tracks laid both by the brontosaur (who was a vegetarian with feet measuring 38 inches across) and by the flesh-eating theropod dinosaurs with three-toed tracks like a chicken.

The tracks of the brontosaur make veritable washtubs, they are so large; and they hold so much water that catfish frequently get caught in them when the river level falls. These dinosaurs had crossed muddy shores looking for food. Later purling water covered the tracks with sand or silt. Then came the sea again, laying new limestone on the old. The sea receded and rivers ran, and in tens of thousands of years the Paluxy wore through the top layers to the basement layer where the tracks were.

That is why today the tracks disappear under layers of limestone. That is why Mr. Connally kept saying, "The old river will turn up new ones even though people steal the ones we see."

People did steal them. They dug out the tracks of solid stone in blocks that weighed several hundred pounds and sold them by the roadside. Today Glen Rose and its dinosaur tracks are

protected by law. Some have already been deposited in museums, the most dramatic being in the New York American Museum of National History.

Dinosaur collectors not only dug out the huge steps from limestone, they also collected polished stones that presumably came from the gizzards of these gargantuan three-toed animals. Doyle Cooper, genial county agricultural agent, told me, "Got buckets full of them thar things."

Some of the tracks of the flesh-eating theropod seem to follow those of the huge brontosaur and one wonders if the former with dragonlike teeth was stalking the bigger vegetarian that it could easily kill were it able to get its long teeth into the snaky neck of its prey.

William B. Cowan, Jr., of the Glen Rose Public School system, issued me a dinosaur hunting license:

DINOSAUR HUNTING LICENSE

SPECIAL PERMIT No. 86-U2869

ISSUED TO:

Name   Justice William O. Douglas

Street   United States Supreme Court

City   Washington, D. C.   State 20543

ISSUED BY AUTHORITY TEXAS REPTILE CONTROL COMMISSION
Restricted to Somervell County, Texas, Only

This license entitles the holder to hunt for, pursue, shoot, kill and remove from the area known as Dinosaur Valley in Somervell County, Texas, which is along the Paluxy River in the vicinity of Glen Rose, Texas, the following types of reptilian wild game:

A. BRONTOSAURUS — 1 only (Adult male)

B. TRACHODON — 1 only (either sex) and weighing not less than 2,000 lbs., live weight

C. ALLOSAURUS — 2 only (without young)

Holder of this license agrees to remove all such game, legally bagged by him under the proper restrictions, properly preserved and in sanitary condition within five (5) days of time of reptile's death, and further agrees to have said game inspected by the Texas Game Warden before removal.

Signed _____

ISSUED BY AL E. OUP

Deputy Lizard Warden and Manager, Glen Rose White Lightning Distilleries, Glen Rose, Texas

(Glen Rose FFA, Young Farmers & Somervell County Historical Society)

A delegation of townfolk (including Judge Temple Summers, Sheriff C. M. Strawn, County Attorney Sam Freas, and D. J. McCarty of the *Glen Rose Reporter,* and John Butner of the *Cleburne Times Review*) went with me as I scouted the river and explored the economy of the county (now built around peanuts, small grasses, and sorghum) and the glories of the Paluxy River which produces large-mouthed bass, channel catfish, and crappies. The Paluxy, which means turkey in the Comanche language, nourishes this land. The river which is a branch of the heavily dammed Brazos is usually sparkling clear. On my visit it was slightly murky, making it difficult to see the submerged dinosaur tracks. It is a river with pools lying below waterfalls that pour over layer after layer of broken limestone, making it seem as one walks upstream that he is climbing a gargantuan stairway.

On our climb a farmer stopped me at a pool to say it was a favorite baptismal spot. He related how a local preacher was baptizing people by submersion one Sunday and found a problem on his hands in the case of one woman who fought vigorously against having her head submerged. As she and the preacher tussled, a countryman shouted from the banks:

"Push her fanny under, mister. That's where all the sin is."

While the Glen Rose territory is farmed, the Edwards Plateau is ranched.

This Plateau was only recently a raw frontier where herds of cattle were gathered for long drives up the trail to Kansas. Cattle went up this trail as late as 1900. The first railroad reached Austin in 1871. On one LBJ ranch that embraces a part of Packsaddle Mountain a historic Indian battle took place on August 4, 1873. Indian raids in the Austin area continued until 1875. No railroad penetrated the Hill Country proper until after the turn of the century.

Ranches—such as the LBJ spread—have farming units where small cereals and corn are grown.

These are the "row crops" in the Hill Country—maize,

sorghum, broom corn, kafir, and any other grain—indeed most produce of the soil except cotton. But those farms are mere islands in a vast range country where cattle, sheep, and goats are run. Many ranchers—perhaps most these days—practice conservation. I have mentioned the "tanks" that have been installed. Management of brush and woodlands has been a problem. If the Plateau were deserted by man it would revert to a climax forest of cedar and oak, with few prairies left. The Indians managed differently. They burned periodically, setting fire to whole sections so that grass would come in and the bison or buffalo would congregate. Thus their meat supply was assured. Burning these days is not practical in view of the enormous hazards. So conservation-minded ranchers plan in a different way. They bulldoze whole sections, piling the debris for burning. These powerful machines uproot oak and cedar. The bee bush (*Aloysia lycioides*) that makes sweet, sweet honey is difficult to bulldoze, as is the black persimmon. These scraggly shrubs tend to come back, over and again. So a circular power mower is used to "shred" them until the grasses take over. The first invaders are weeds. But as they are annuals, the hardier grasses take over in a year or so. These are not the tall grasses of the plains, such as the big bluestem and Indian grass; the grasses of the Edwards Plateau are short ones—various species of grama grasses, muhly, and the like. (There are about 700 grasses in Texas, half of all there are in the entire United States. And a goodly number are in the Hill Country.)

A rancher does not bulldoze the entire land. He saves cedar "breaks" for livestock, especially for goats that are sensitive to cold when first sheared.

This cedar is juniper, usually one of two species. It is the only timber of importance on the Plateau being used mainly for fence posts, the hill people who cut it for posts being called "cedar choppers." The gum of cedar is sometimes chewed with the stretch berry and children find it a fair substitute for bubble gum.

The farmer usually saves portions of his woods for deer. The white-tailed deer flourishes here and given browse and wooded protection thrives.

"Deer involve no investment," one rancher told me. "It's our best cash crop."

Ranchers on the Edwards Plateau are following the example of those in West Texas and rent or lease their lands for deer hunting. These fees are, indeed, important cash items in the economy of the area.

Nearly half of all our wild turkeys are found in Texas, principally in the Edwards Plateau; and there is fossil evidence that they are one of Texas' oldest inhabitants. I have seen them strutting the ridges, with as many as a half-dozen gobblers out in front.

Ranching usually involves running cattle, sheep, and goats on the same range at the same time.

"Cattle eat the tops, sheep eat farther down, and goats clean out brush," is the way one rancher justified it. Some ranches are woefully overgrazed. Properly managed pastures on one side of a road show rich grass mixed with a myriad of flowers, while on the other side the hoofs of sheep and goat have so pounded the turf as to destroy it. When that happens a mint takes over (*Salvia farinacea*) that even sheep and goats will not eat.

"Sheep and goats must be hard on the land," I said to one rancher.

"In small numbers they are good for it," he replied.

"Why?"

"They kill a snake by jumping on its head with all four feet cupped together."

Most of the Edwards Plateau was once overgrazed, and that overgrazing has left a legacy. For example, in large areas quail have become scarce.

The Plateau has an average rainfall of only 28 inches to 30 inches a year. The 1960s have been wet; the 1950s were dry. When the grasses are in short supply, even the edible weeds thin out. But unless the land is pressed too hard by overpopulation, livestock survives. One important plant is the *Evax prolisera* that sheep ignore in lush days and relish in times of drought. The prickly pear is the old reliable for cattle. A portable butane tank is used to throw a six-foot flame that burns off the dry spines of the plant, making it edible for cows. The prickly pear, which is scattered widespread across the Plateau, carried many a rancher through the drought of the 1950s.

"It got so that some old cows wouldn't eat anything but *warm* prickly pears," one rancher told me. "They followed me and my butane flame around like puppy dogs."

Ranching that uses conservation methods has increased the beauty of the Plateau by creating open grasslands lined with the dark green of cedars and oaks and the light green of walnuts.

Scattered clumps of yucca are everywhere. Spanish bayonet is very much on display. The bull nettle, attractive to the eye but poisonous to human touch, lines many roadways. The evening primrose shows golden yellow.

Some ranches look like parks, and near sunset abound with deer. At dusk on Riley Mountain in the area known as the Red Farm I have seen more than a hundred white tails in a half-hour. This mountaintop has cool springs and it was once farmed. Old fields of the red-clay soil still show their outlines, the grasses are still luxuriant, and the cedar "breaks" are thick.

Riley Mountain adjoins Packsaddle Mountain, so named because its lowest pass is a perfect outline of a saddle. The top of Packsaddle is rocky but passable. The top of Riley Mountain is easier going. As I stood there in the twilight, I thought how wonderful it would be if both of those mountains were on a trail system where saddle horses and hikers could travel. There are no such trails of any consequence in the Plateau. Ranching would not interfere with them, as it would be necessary to acquire only easements for their use. The trail system could follow the ridges and yet never lie far from springs. Shelters could be erected and fireplaces built so that overnight facilities would be available. I see in my mind's eye a trail system of several hundred miles with spurs down lateral ridges. I see this trail system linking up with trails along some of the rivers. The Guadalupe River below Canyon Dam and above New Braunfels is an ideal candidate. The pitch of the valley is a gentle one. The trail would be in deep shade most of the way, shade produced by majestic pecan trees and by huge cypress (*Taxodium distichum*). It would skirt the base of 100-foot to 200-foot limestone cliffs that are very reminiscent of the famous Buffalo River in the Ozarks. It would cross a few rich open bottom lands (whose soil is the product of oxidation of lime) and lead to attractive camp sites.

Other river valleys and other ridges could become important trailways for saddle horses and for back-packers. Surveys and studies need be made by men and women as expert as those who make up the Appalachian Mountain Club in New England, the Green Mountain Club in Vermont, and the Sierra Club in California. The Sierra has the John Muir Trail; New Hampshire has the White Mountain Trail System integrated with alpine huts managed by the Appalachian Mountain Club; and the Green Mountains have the Long Trail.

Come winter, there are freezes and some snow falls high up. The snakes have retired for the season. Then is the time for apartment-bred man to escape the city and spend part of his winter seeing the glories of the Plateau on foot or horseback and reliving the days of the Comanches and the white settlers and seeing for himself the wonders of acorn forests and pecan bottom lands. The trail system of the Plateau should become the

Lyndon B. Johnson Trail. He has traveled and hunted areas that
will make up parts of it. Beyond that is the fact that this is "a
President's Country," as Jack R. Maguire has described it in
his book by that name.

The planning for recreational use should go much further.
Trails for hikers and saddle horses tap only parts of the potential.
There are sites almost without number that could be integrated into a park system, offering families a week or two of
travel with a different camp site each night and with climbing,
bird watching, botanizing, swimming, or fishing as diversions
from the humdrum of life. Glen Rose and its dinosaur sanctuary
are a good place to start. Private owners now charge a fee to
see these sights. But there are no campground facilities. At
Enchanted Rock the proprietors have nice camp facilities. But
the entire area should be acquired and the facilities enlarged so
that auto and trailer use is increased a hundredfold. The ridge
and slopes commanded by the Balanced Rock should be made
into a park complex. Large picnic and campground acreages
should be acquired along the Guadalupe and other rivers. Many
of the springs I have mentioned are privately owned and offer
only limited facilities. These should be obtained and extended.
The lovely Prade Ranch at the head of the Frio River, embracing more than 8,000 acres, should be under public custody and
protected against the vagaries of private ownership.

With planning, a complex of parks—state and Federal—unequaled in any state could be designed for the Plateau; and it
appropriately should be called the LBJ Park System.

When the President first showed me the Hill Country in the
late thirties, few practiced conservation. That has greatly changed
with the arrival of AAA and its several agencies. The present
despoilers of the Hill Country are the minority that still look
with disdain on conservation measures. Their lands are depleted
even in the eye of the amateur. To them the land has never
become sacred; it is there to use like a paper cup and then dis-

carded. The concept of a renewable resource—the lesson the AAA tried to inculcate more than 30 years ago—is still foreign to some people of the Hill Country. They can perhaps in time be educated.

The greatest threat to the Hill Country comes from entrepreneurs in water. West Texas is dry and thirsty. The Hill Country is green and wet. Its rivers and its springs are its very life blood. Texas to date, however, gives no protection to that water supply. Adventurers can come in and drill wherever they like and transport the water wherever they choose. Theoretically, they can suck the Edwards Plateau dry; there is at present no law to stop them. That is why the Edwards Plateau Underground Water District has not gone forward with its plans to build dams that will recharge the aquifers.

"Why should we sell bond issues and saddle ourselves with debt when a West Texas promoter might come in and pump out our aquifers?" one district official asked me.

The lines are being formed for a tremendous water struggle in Texas. Out-of-basin diversions are being hotly debated—their ethics and propriety, and their economics as well. This is the first true conservation issue that Texas has faced. The Texas legislature tried to stop the transportation of percolating waters out of the state. A city in Oklahoma bought subsurface water rights from a Texas farmer and undertook to bring the water across state lines for its municipal purposes. A Federal court in 1966 upheld the project, ruling that the ban which Texas put on that transportation was an unconstitutional burden on interstate commerce (255 F. Supp. 828). As a result of that ruling, the problem of out-of-state diversions shifts to Congress that can sanction them or ban them as it sees fit. Yet while Texas seeks to stop out-of-state diversions of water, it clamors for interstate shipments of water into West Texas from the Colorado, the Missouri, the Mississippi, and even the Columbia rivers. She is now pressing those claims before Congress.

Texans dedicated to the land, to wild life, to trees, grasses, and flowers—Texans who want trails and parks for recreation—Texans who want clean waterways—Texans who share the passion for conservation that Thoreau and Muir knew—these men and women are numerous. Their voices are beginning to be heard. But they have not yet won many battles. The Big Bend National Park—wondrous as it is—was not a mark of Texas dedication to conservation. It succeeded because it "bailed out" ranchers who by overgrazing had turned rich land into a dollarless desert. Plain greed, not idealism, gave birth to that park. The creation of the Guadalupe National Park was a different story; and it may mark a turning point.

Yet whether the modern Ahabs can be unseated remains to be seen.

They see a tree and think in terms of board feet.

They see a cliff and think in terms of gravel.

They see a river and think in terms of dams, because dams mean profitable contracts, don't they?

They see a mountain and think in terms of minerals, roads, and excavations.

They think of parks in terms of private enterprise—money-making schemes—not nature trails, but amusement centers.

Recreation is coming to be one of our major problems, and it will increase in intensity as our population soon doubles. Texas is mostly not concerned.

Texas thinks not in terms of the wonders of baygalls and the glories of bayous. Those water wonders are either mere building sites for real-estate promoters and construction companies or open sewers for the easy use of cities such as Houston.

In the six years it took me to complete the field work for this volume I heard every outdoor value I know appraised largely in terms of dollars. All except one—the wonderful sunsets of Texas. And I left Texas convinced that somewhere some promoter probably had plans for them, too.

The only hope lies in young ranchers such as Don McIvor; in oilmen such as Mr. Pratt and Mr. Hunter; in the men in Texas' politics such as Ralph W. Yarborough, Wright Patman, and Dempsie Henley, who are awake to the problems of conservation and are determined to do something about them; in courageous newspaper people; in men such as Lance Rosier, Peter Koch, Justice Jim Bowmer, and Bob Burleson; in small but growing organizations that are arousing the citizens; and in people such as Lyndon B. Johnson and Lady Bird.

But when it comes to saving the wilderness, these people are in the minority, which makes the conservationists of Texas a lonely lot. Conservationists the nation over will, however, join them in fighting the great battles that lie ahead. But the modern Ahabs are more strongly entrenched in Texas than anywhere else.

That is why this is a melancholy book. That is why when we think of conservation, nature trails, back-packing, camping, and outdoor recreation, we must say FAREWELL TO TEXAS— unless the dedicated minority receives an overwhelming mandate from the people.

APPENDIX

This catalogue of ferns and orchids of the Big Thicket area
was prepared for me by Dr. Donovan S. Correll.

Ferns and Fern Allies Found in the Big Thicket and in Southeast Texas

Asplenium platyneuron (L.) Oakes—Ebony Spleenwort

Athyrium filix-femina (L.) Roth var. asplenioides (Michx.) Farw.—
Southern Lady-fern

Azolla caroliniana Willd.—Mosquito-fern

Botrychium dissectum Spreng. var. tenuifolium (Underw.) Farw.—
Cut-leaved Grape-fern

Botrychium virginianum (L.) Sw.—Virginia Rattlesnake Fern

Cheilanthes alabamensis (Buckl.) Kunze—Alabama Lipfern

Equisetum laevigatum A. Br.—Smooth Scouring-rush

Equisetum prealtum Raf.—Tall Scouring-rush

Isoetes melanopoda Gay & Durieu—Black-foot Quillwort

Lorinseria areolata (L.) Presl.—Chain-fern

Lycopodium adpressum (Chapm.) Lloyd & Underw.—Southern Club-
moss

Lycopodium alopecuroides L.—Foxtail Club-moss

Lycopodium carolinianum L.—Carolina Club-moss

Lygodium japonicum (Thunb.) Sw.—Japanese Climbing-fern

Nephrolepis exaltata (L.) Schott—Sword-fern

Onoclea sensibilis L.—Sensitive-fern

Ophioglossum Engelmannii Prantl—Engelmann's Adder's-tongue

Ophioglossum vulgatum L.—Common Adder's-tongue

Osmunda cinnamomea L.—Cinnamon Fern

Osmunda regalis L. var. spectabilis (Willd.) Gray—Royal Fern

Polypodium polypodioides (L.) Watt. var. Michauxianum Weatherby—
Resurrection-fern

Polystichum acrostichoides (Michx.) Schott—Christmas-fern

Psilotum nudum (L.) Griseb.—Whisk-fern

Pteridium aquilinum (L.) Kuhn var. pseudocaudatum (Clute) Heller—
Bracken-fern

Selaginella apoda (L.) Fern.—Meadow Spike-moss

Selaginella Riddellii Van Eseltine—Riddell's Spike-moss

Thelypteris dentata (Forsk.) E. St. John—Downy Shield-fern

Thelypteris hexagonoptera (Michx.) Weatherby—Broad Beech-fern
Thelypteris normalis (C. Chr.) Moxley—Southern Shield-fern
Thelypteris setigera Blume—Hairy Shield-fern
Thelypteris palustris var. Haleana Fern.—Marsh-fern
Thelypteris versicolor R. P. St. John—St. John's Shield-fern
Woodsia obtusa (Spreng.) Torr.—Common Woodsia
Woodwardia virginica (L.) J. Sm.—Virginia Chain-fern

Orchids Found in the Big Thicket and in Southeast Texas

Calopogon barbatus (Walt.) Ames—Bearded Grass-pink
Calopogon pulchellus (Salisb.) R. Br.—Grass-pink
Cleistes divaricata (L.) Ames—Spreading Pogonia
Corallorhiza Wisteriana Conrad—Wister's Coral-root
Erythrodes querceticola (Lindl.) Ames—Low Erythrodes
Habenaria blephariglottis (Willd.) Hook.—White Fringe-orchid
Habenaria Chapmanii (Small) Ames—Chapman's Fringe-orchid
Habenaria ciliaris (L.) R. Br.—Yellow Fringe-orchid
Habenaria clavellata (Michx.) Spreng.—Green Woodland Orchid
Habenaria cristata (Michx.) R. Br.—Crested Fringe-orchid
Habenaria flava (L.) R. Br.—Tubercled Fringe-orchid
Habenaria integra (Nutt.) Spreng.—Orange Rein-orchid
Habenaria nivea (Nutt.) Spreng.—Snowy Orchid; Bog Torch
Habenaria quinqueseta (Michx.) Sw.—Pine Rein-orchid
Habenaria repens Nutt.—Creeping Orchid
Isotria verticillata (Muhl.) Raf.—Whorled Pogonia
Listera australis Lindl.—Southern Twayblade
Malaxis unifolia Michx.—Green Adder's Mouth
Pogonia ophioglossoides (L.) Ker-Gawl.—Rose Pogonia
Ponthieva racemosa (Walt.) Mohr—Shadow-witch
Spiranthes cernua (L.) L. C. Rich.—Nodding Ladies' Tresses
Spiranthes cernua var. odorata (Nutt.) Correll—Fragrant Ladies' Tresses
Spiranthes gracilis (Bigel.) Beck—Slender Ladies' Tresses
Spiranthes Grayi Ames—Gray's Ladies' Tresses
Spiranthes laciniata (Small) Ames—Fringe-lip Ladies' Tresses
Spiranthes praecox (Walt.) Wats.—Grass-leaved Ladies' Tresses
Spiranthes vernalis Engelm. & Gray—Spring Ladies' Tresses
Tipularia discolor (Pursh) Nutt.—Crane-fly Orchid
Triphora trianthophora (Sw.) Rydb.—Nodding Pogonia

INDEX